The Mobile Technology Question and Answer Book

A Survival Guide for Business Managers

Ron Schneiderman

AMACOM

American Management Association

New York • Atlanta • Brussels • Buenos Aires • Chicago • London • Mexico City
San Francisco • Shanghai • Tokyo • Toronto • Washington, D.C.

Special discounts on bulk quantities of AMACOM books are available to corporations, professional associations, and other organizations. For details, contact Special Sales Department, AMACOM, a division of American Management Association, 1601 Broadway, New York, NY 10019. Tel.: 212-903-8316. Fax: 212-903-8083. Web site: www.amacombooks.org

This publication is designed to provide accurate and authoritative information in regard to the subject matter covered. It is sold with the understanding that the publisher is not engaged in rendering legal, accounting, or other professional service. If legal advice or other expert assistance is required, the services of a competent professional person should be sought.

Library of Congress Cataloging-in-Publications data has been applied for and is on record at the Library of Congress.

Printing number
10 9 8 7 6 5 4 3 2 1

Contents

Introduction

Getting away from it all is getting tougher. Soon, it may be impossible. Cellular phones, satellite phones, handheld computers, and personal navigation systems capable of pinpointing your location within a few feet are all becoming connected through new generations of wireless services and the Internet. Anyone can now reach you virtually anywhere, and at anytime. And the engineers who design these totally mobile devices are just getting warmed up. Mobile devices are getting smaller and lighter, and they offer more features than ever before. This trend is likely to continue with the introduction of more accessorized and highly integrated products.

What do you need, and what do you need to know to be more efficient while away from your home or office? What products and services are currently available to make your life easier, and your business more productive? And what will the next generation of these tools look like? Most of the answers are in this book.

But first, a little history.

We all know that Alexander Graham Bell invented the telephone (he received patent no. 174,465 just 125 years ago, in 1876), and that Guglielmo Marconi transmitted the first "wireless" message across the Atlantic Ocean in 1901.

Less interesting, perhaps, is the fact that the Federal Communications Commission (FCC) was established in 1934, when Congress passed the Communications Act to regulate interstate communications. However, the FCC, and this single piece of legislation, have played critical roles in the technical development and growth of telecommunications worldwide.

There were only about 200 million telephones in use in the world in 1967, fewer than there are cellular phones in use in the United States alone today. That was also the year that cordless telephones were introduced.

The following year, the U.S. Supreme Court changed the entire industry almost overnight with its highly contentious Carterfone decision, essentially eliminating AT&T's historical control of the public telephone network in the United States. The Carterfone was a special device developed by Tom Carter, a Texas-based small-business telecom equipment entrepreneur. It was designed to protect the Bell network from any "foreign" equipment, but AT&T argued that no equipment should be attached to its network but its own. The court's ruling allowed, for the first time, the interconnection of non-Bell equipment to the Bell telephone network—a decision that led to an almost immediate proliferation of new telecom equipment for business and residential users from a variety of manufacturers, many of them based outside the United States.

Another historical moment in the telecom industry's history was the successful launch of Sputnik by the USSR in 1957. The "space race" that almost immediately followed between the United States and the Soviet Union led to the formation of the Advanced Research Project Agency, or ARPA, whose role was to help the United States catch up to the USSR in space, and eventually to surpass it.

Working in mostly unmarked office buildings in and around Washington, D.C., ARPA took on top secret, high-priority R&D projects under the direction and management of the Pentagon. (ARPA later became the Defense Advanced Research Project Agency, or DARPA.) One of these projects was the development of a communications system that would be independent of the Bell system and could therefore be protected if the United States were ever attacked by a foreign power. If part of the communications system was knocked out in one part of the country, the system would still be in operation in other critical areas.

Linking computers through this vast, dedicated communications network would allow scientists, engineers, and others to share information, not only more efficiently than in the past, but faster. It became known as the ARPAnet.

The ARPAnet was launched in 1967, connecting computers in Massachusetts and California. By 1971, more than forty computers were linked across the country. At about the same time, ARPAnet users began experimenting with an electronic mail program that enabled them to share messages and data files. Over the next several years, the practice of sending messages and ever-larger data files over this growing computer network began to shift from strictly military use to use by universities and corporations.

By 1982 it had become clear to its users that the ARPAnet could not grow and continue to be useful if its basic elements were incompatible, as was true of the computers on the system. It also became obvious that if the ARPAnet was going to expand, everyone using it would have to sign on to a common protocol. That came, in time, with the development of the Transmission Control Protocol/Internet Protocol, or TCP/IP, which became the standard operating procedure for what is now widely known as, simply, the Internet.

Within five years, more than 5,000 computers were "online" around the world. That number jumped to more than 100,000 by 1989. By 1995, three million computers were tied into the Internet. Today, there are more than 150 million Internet users in the United States alone, and nearly that many in the rest of the world. And the number of users is growing fast, so much so that the market research organization Strategy Analytics is projecting that the global market for mobile wireless Internet-capable devices—including handheld computers, microbrowser-based mobile phones, and next-generation multimedia phones—will jump from $10 billion in 2000 to $73 billion in 2005. Much of this growth will result from a dramatic shift in the price/performance equation during that time, as well as from meeting the growing need of mobile device users for information, communication, and entertainment. In other words, demand will continue to grow as the price drops and the performance of these devices improves.

Clearly, the ability to remotely send and receive e-mail, search an office directory, get weather reports, make airline and hotel reservations, handle banking and other financial transactions, access mobile customer relationship management (CRM) tools and sales force support, and access procurement facilities and management reporting information, as well as managing many other fast-emerging business functions, is creating virtual offices for business managers and other professionals everywhere.

About This Book

The explosion of both the Internet and wireless technologies has led to totally new industries and markets, created thousands of companies, and probably millions of new jobs. It has also opened whole new vistas and challenges for business managers, who must now find ways of integrating these technologies into their businesses. As more mobile products and services become available to the business community and to consumers, a business will have trouble competing for customers if it cannot be accessed from anywhere at anytime.

- What products and services are available to you and your business?

- How will mobile technologies make your business more productive and, therefore, more competitive?

- What regulatory issues are involved in the development of mobile technologies?

- What are some of the unresolved issues still facing the mobile communication and computing industries?

Tell Me More

Those questions are just a jumping-off point for what is currently happening in mobile communications and computing. The total number of mobile phone sold worldwide will have reached an estimated 490 million in 2001. The introduction of next-generation mobile phones and other wireless devices will more than double that number in unit sales in the next year or two.

It is the goal of this book to provide you with a comprehensive understanding of mobile technologies, and why they are important to you in your work. The first chapter, "Mobile Basics," is just that, an explanation of the basics of mobile technologies and how mobile products, services, and applications may be applied to your business. It also defines some of the key elements of these new and emerging mobile technologies that apply specifically to the business community.

The second chapter of the book, "Mobile Internet and Data Services," defines the mobile Internet and explores in some detail the business applications and services that are available today. Chapter 3, "Software and Protocols," delves into the rapidly emerging wireless programs and technical standards that make mobile communications work. It also discusses developments that are underway to ensure that the technology and the market continue to grow on a relatively smooth path.

Chapter 4, "Software-Defined Radio," takes a look at a fast emerging technology that may soon change the way mobile phones and other wireless devices are designed, serviced, and used. In Chapter 5, "Messaging Services," the various types of messaging services available to the business/professional user—from traditional paging to instant messaging and Multimedia Message Service—are described in detail. Chapter 6, "Mobile Devices, Services, and Special Features," discusses how mobile phones and personal digital assistants (PDAs) fit into the mobile mix, and it also covers peripheral technologies and services that could become very important to the business user.

Chapter 7, "Cellular Communications and Specialized Mobile Radio," provides a good background in cellular communications, and explains where Specialized Mobile Radio (SMR) fits into the menu of mobile technology services. Chapter 8, "Location-Based Services," discusses the technology and services that enable location-specific information to be delivered to mobile devices, including telematics, E-911, and satellite-based navigation systems.

Chapter 9, "Mobile Commerce Applications," looks at mobile shopping, wireless advertising, and methods for applying mobile technologies to business and personal financial transactions and banking, and reviews current activities in broader mobile commerce issues, including retailing. Chapter 10, "Security and Privacy Issues," offers a critical description of the security and privacy issues you should be concerned about. It also discusses how smart cards, PC cards, and private networks fit into the development and application of mobile technologies. Chapter 11, "Electronic Payments," covers the development and status of digital signatures and other operating rules and business practices in this new and fast-emerging e-wallet environment.

The final chapter of the book, Chapter 12, "Next-Generation Systems...and Beyond," describes how today's wireless technologies are expected to migrate to the next round of applications and mobile technologies. It also lays out the critical issues surrounding current developments in Third- and Fourth Generation (3G and 4G) mobile communications.

Each chapter in the book consists of several questions and answers. The answers are followed by bullet points that highlight key facts or issues surrounding the question. For readers wishing to know the details of a particular issue, more complete information is given under the heading "Tell Me More." In the back of the book, there is an extensive glossary, which defines and explains many of the terms and acronyms used in the book.

The wide-ranging questions and detailed answers presented in the twelve chapters are designed to give you a good basic understanding of how mobile technologies could impact the future of your business and its operations.

Acknowledgments

I would like to thank my acquisitions editor at AMACOM, Jacqueline Flynn, without who's encouragement ("You're not going to get any sympathy from me; a deadline is a deadline") this book might never have been completed.

I would also like to thank my mother-in-law, Ceil Edwin, who, on regular calls to her in Florida would inquire, "How many words did you write today?" Also, my grandson, Jonah Benjamin Schneiderman. He can't type yet, but I have to believe that by the time he's old enough to use some of the technologies described in this book, he probably won't have to.

Chapter 1

Mobile Basics

1.1 What is mobile commerce?

Unlike electronic commerce (e-commerce), which normally requires desktop computers to connect to the Internet and send and receive e-mail, mobile commerce (m-commerce) offers the added benefit of mobility that makes conducting business or making a purchase via the Internet an anywhere, anytime e-commerce experience. Simply put, m-commerce provides consumers with the ability to obtain information and order goods and services quickly and easily via the Internet using a wireless device.

- For most consumers, the m-commerce experience means location-based services and wireless over-the-counter purchases.

- Interest in m-commerce has generally been slow; however, that should change with the development of new applications and advances for devices and software.

Tell Me More

Although few people are likely to buy a house or a boat using their mobile device, other types of wireless transactions are gaining in popularity. Some analysts expect m-commerce to generate revenues in the $200 billion-plus range by 2006.

M-commerce applications are likely to include business- and consumer-driven location-based services, from information on finding restaurants, movie theaters, concerts, and retail centers, to such services as banking, online shopping, vending/parking machine payments, electronic ticketing, and wireless point-of-sale purchases. To help support the development and maintenance of these services, wireless carriers are expected to sell advertising, sometimes in the form of simple but well-recognized logos that would appear on the display screens of cellular phones and other mobile devices.

Interest in m-commerce by wireless carriers and businesses is developing relatively slowly. However, many carriers are in the process of launching or testing m-commerce services, and a growing number of businesses, particularly retailers and restaurants, have begun field testing wireless technologies to help grow and differentiate their organizations. Several trials were underway during 2001, including tests at Domino's Pizza and Starbuck's Coffee.

The real estate industry is another good candidate for mobile commerce. Real Estate Connect, the industry's largest technology conference, has become a showcase for wireless applications. However, OnePipeline is believed to be the only national company so far that allows real estate brokers, agents, and builders to directly initiate the mortgage loan process for their clients using wireless technologies. (Much more detailed information on mobile retailing/shopping and other examples of m-commerce appear later in Chapter 8.)

Part of the reason for the slow uptake in m-commerce has been due to consumer expectations. Many wireless subscribers want to literally duplicate their desktop PC experience in the mobile environment. Currently, that is not always possible.

Part of the problem, according to a number of analysts, has been to convince end users that m-commerce is a complement to e-commerce, not a substitute. Also, most m-commerce purchases will be low-ticket items, not cars and furniture. However, the rapid development of mobile technologies (high-speed data transmission, data security, ease-of-use features, new applications, and improved interfaces (such as displays, keyboards, and speech recognition systems) should boost interest in m-commerce and help drive its growth. Any number of applications are in the works, from online mobile learning (foreign languages, etc.) to play-for-pay downloadable games and other entertainment.

1.2 What is the future of mobile technologies?[1]

With the number of mobile phones approaching one billion globally, the opportunities for equipment manufacturers, service providers, and users are tremendous. Market projections vary widely, but most analysts agree that at least half of all mobile devices used for Internet access will eventually also be used for mobile commerce, including business-to-business (B2B) and business-to-consumer (B2C) applications. Most of the trends being projected are very ambitious.

- Several very heady projections have been made about the near- and long-term growth of mobile technologies.

- The number of wireless data users in North America will grow dramatically by 2004, with wireless data users outnumbering wireline subscribers.

- Worldwide, more than 1.5 billion mobile devices will be wireless-enabled by 2004.

Tell Me More

In some areas, data traffic is almost equal to wireline voice traffic. Also, even though mobile traffic has been estimated at barely more than 2 percent in the United States, at least one in-depth market study indicates that nearly half of mobile phone subscribers have Internet access at home through desktop PCs. The assumption is that as more people gain access to the Internet—from home or office—they will extend this capability into the mobile environment, and mobile traffic on the Internet will increase rapidly.

Several very heady projections have been made about the growth of mobile technologies in the workplace over the next several years. For example, it was forecast that in the next four years, more than one-third of the United States working population will be "mobile professionals," and that 50 percent of Fortune 1000 companies expect to commit 15 percent of all networking services spending to wireless voice and data solutions by 2004.

Wireless access is expected to evolve dramatically between now and 2004. Devices and standards continue to proliferate. In addition, 35 percent of knowledge workers will rely on a mix of three or more devices (laptop computers, mobile phones, personal digital assistants, etc.) during the business day.

The number of mobile phones is expected to surpass landlines by 2004. By 2005, there will probably be more than one billion mobile phone users worldwide. Globally, 240 million people are expected to use their phones for wireless data exchange by the end of 2004—up from 26 million in 1999. The growth of the global mobile data market is projected at 75 percent annually and is expected to be worth $80 billion by 2005.

In addition, 40 percent of mobile workers will be compelled to carry technologies that offer instant response by voice and hourly response by e-mail, and 70 percent of new wireless phones will offer that service. Also, 40 percent of new PDAs will have direct access to Web content and enterprise networks.

The ability to aggregate and manipulate data from multiple sources and deliver effective content efficiently is paramount, and it is the true measure of success for an enterprise information system.

North America. The number of wireless data users will climb rapidly from 5.7 million in 2000 to more than 70 million in 2004. There will be at least 100 million subscribers using some form of mobile data by 2007.

Analysts estimate that just 2 percent of mobile traffic was data at the end of 2000.

Currently, there are 40 million mobile professionals in the United States requiring constant access to e-mail, corporate intranets, inventory, and various online services.

Worldwide. By the year 2005, 484 million people will access the Internet via wireless technology. In fact, forecasts for PDA sales in Western Europe call for an increase of from 2.5 million units in 2001 to more than 6.5 million in 2004, representing a 47 percent yearly growth rate. Revenues for wireless e-mail applications in Europe are also expected to grow dramatically, reaching $7 billion in 2004.

European analysts are projecting that 50 percent of wireless revenues in 2010 will be from nonvoice applications.

1.3 Are the predictions of growth for mobile technologies just hype?

Wireless data and the mobile Internet have been among the most hyped technologies in recent history. Market projections for the deployment of these systems are impressive; however, the reality is that it may take another two to three years, perhaps longer, to reach the numbers that are currently being projected by independent market analysts. Similarly, the rapid growth in revenue from m-commerce transactions is not expected to take place until after 2004.

- Nearly half the United States workforce currently has access to Web-enabled wireless devices on the job.

- The complexity of the technology could slow the growth of wireless data and Internet applications.

- M-commerce users could climb to 91 million by 2007.

- The driver for mobile data and m-commerce will be more highly miniaturized, higher-speed, and easier-to-use mobile devices.

Tell Me More

By the end of 2001, nearly half of the U.S. workforce will have access to Web-enabled wireless devices on the job, and if market projections hold up, 60 percent of all U.S. employees will be using wireless devices by 2004. In some parts of the world, particularly in areas where all-digital service is more mature than in the United States—for example, in Scandinavia and Japan—the numbers are much higher.

However, the complexity of the technology, the hard-to-read tiny screens, the dearth of truly useful applications, and the relatively high cost are likely to hold wireless data traffic and m-commerce to relatively moderate levels over the next few years, probably somewhat off the numbers projected in mid-2000 by many independent market research organizations.

Analysts see increasing numbers of m-commerce users as the engine of revenue growth. And although The Strategis Group, a market research organization with a special interest in mobile technologies, says it anticipates fewer than 1 million m-commerce users in the United States by year-end of 2001, it projects that number to climb rapidly to more than 91 million by 2007. To do that, however, end users must be convinced that m-commerce is a complement, not a substitute, for the much more accessible and easier-to-navigate features of desktop PC accessible e-commerce. Realistically, consumers will not use their mobile phones or PDAs to buy cars or furniture. Most m-commerce will be relatively low-end purchases by people on the move.

The driver for turning mobile data and m-commerce into a mass market and major enterprise investment will be the development and introduction of smaller, lighter, high-speed, and easy-to-use mobile devices. Products that fit the bill are currently in design and development.

1.4 What is the future of mobile data at this point?

Despite the slowing of cellular phone sales in late 2000 and into 2001, the outlook for the mobile devices market continues to be strong over the long term. For the foreseeable future, voice and messaging will continue to be the most popular applications worldwide (although messaging is much more popular in Europe and Japan than in the United States, at least for now). This should begin to change beginning in 2003 or 2004, when most devices that tap into the Internet for data will no longer be PCs; rather, they will be portable wireless devices.

The ability to access corporate and personal databases will be a major factor in the development and growth of mobile data applications. Virtually all industries will benefit from this technology. An obvious example is real estate where wireless technologies are driving change and creating new opportunities for flexibility and convenient access to the Internet and their own network applications.

- Global cell phone sales are expected to rise 17 percent annually through 2005.

- The mobile data market is expected to reach 60 percent penetration in the United States by 2007.

- Most of the mobile data growth is coming from high-speed networks.

- Expect a huge jump in U.S. wireless Web use over the next few years.

Tell Me More

Market projections by the consulting group Strategy Analytics indicate that global cellular handset shipments will grow at 17 percent annually through 2005. Most of these phones will be replacement models in North America and Western Europe, so this does not represent a pure increase in mobile phone use. It does, however, mean that mobile voice and data traffic will very likely increase with more people using their mobile phones and other wireless devices for business, and to access the Internet and their e-mail.

Another market research organization, The Strategis Group, expects at least 60 percent of the U.S. population to be using the data features of their mobile phones and other wireless devices by 2007, up from two percent at the end of 2000. Much of this growth is attributed to the aggressive deployment of high-speed services in the United States.

Much of the growth in mobile data will be over today's dominant wireless providers, such as Nextel and AT&T Wireless. Nextel Communications has already launched a high-speed data network, and the launch of digital PocketNet service and the availability of two-way Short

Message Service (SMS) on digital networks will accelerate mobile data usage.

Outlook for Wireless Web Users. The number of U.S. wireless Web users will jump from just over four million in 2000 to 96 million in 2005, according to market intelligence specialist Jupiter Media Metrix. Of the 96 million, 75 million are expected to use voice-centric handsets (wireless phones for the most part), 7.3 million will use data-capable handsets, and 4.4 million will use wireless PDAs.

Because of its higher level of functionality (mainly higher data transmission speeds), the adoption of third generation (3G) mobile networks is expected to provide a major boost for mobile data applications and use. However, while 3G is likely to be widespread in Japan within two years, companies focusing on the U.S. and European markets may have to wait three to four years to see any significant market penetration of this next-generation technology.

1.5 Are mobile information technologies being adopted by the IT community?

With certain noteworthy application-driven exceptions, the IT community has been slow to adopt mobile technologies. Surveys indicate that relatively few corporate IT departments in the United States have developed full-blown mobile service programs. However, a growing number of companies indicate that they are building this capability into their IT departments, or are investigating the need for this capability.

- Wireless applications are becoming standard operating procedure in corporate data centers.

- Half of IT managers expect to begin using mobile technologies by the end of 2001.

- Many companies do not have m-commerce plans.

- IT professionals are already among the most "connected" in business.

Tell Me More

Wireless applications have already become standard operating procedure in one of four corporate data centers, creating a need for new software, additional storage requirements for data developed mainly outside the traditional workplace, and increased demand for consulting services, according to a study by AFCOM's Data Center Institute, an association of data center professionals. By the beginning of 2002, more than 40 percent of IT departments will have implemented a wireless strategy, according to the survey.

InternetWeek reported in early 2001 that some 76 percent of the IT and business managers it surveyed in late 2000 indicated they were not yet using wireless Web technology, mainly because of a lack of security, a lack of reliable standards, or inadequate bandwidth. However, at least half of these respondents said they expect their companies to begin using mobile technologies by the end of 2001. And although most companies are ready to make a significant investment in mobile wireless devices, there is a growing concern among IT managers about keeping their systems secure as they begin to connect these devices to their companies' internal networks, or to the Internet.

M-commerce is a similar story in terms of acceptance of the technology. There are always early adopters, but most companies that have not yet started planning m-commerce programs give several reasons, including not having a budget to develop m-commerce applications, a lack of skilled employees to develop the applications, little top-level support, and having to concentrate on other areas. Also, whereas many companies believe m-commerce is still an unproven technology, they recognize that they cannot afford to sit back and wait for the technology to mature. In fact, several surveys conducted during 2001 indicate that a growing number of large and mid-size companies will adopt mobile technologies and develop m-commerce programs over the next few years. Most of these companies will focus on business-to-business applications, and they will create business-to-consumer programs where appropriate.

IT professionals are not above the fray. An online poll conducted by TechRepublic in early 2001 disclosed that 75 percent of the IT professionals responding to the question, "How successful are you at balancing your professional (and personal) life?" said they're not successful or only somewhat successful in finding this balance. One of the problems, according to TechRepublic's analysis of its survey data, is that IT pros are, like doctors, among the most "connected" of all professionals, always tied into a wireless network with cellphones and pagers and—in the case of the IT people—laptop computers. "Technology makes the office always within easy reach for them. Most IT pros don't want to carry their inbox on their belt. But it is getting harder [for them] to leave the office."

1.6 What do I need to consider when developing a corporate mobile strategy?

IT managers face several issues in developing a corporate mobile strategy.

- The difficulty of connecting mobile devices to companies' internal networks

- Higher support costs for mobile users

- The effect on performance of widespread mobile use

- Technical standards and compatibility issues

- The new hardware and software required by mobile technologies

- The development of a clear business strategy for adopting mobile technologies

- The need to develop and implement security systems for corporate wireless networks

Tell Me More

For a variety of reasons (such as staffing, new product turnover, software updates, applications development, and help desk requirements), support costs will be higher for mobile users, at least in the initial stage. The Gartner Group, a leading consultancy and market research organization, estimates that support costs for mobile users are 40 percent higher than those of desktop PC users. Gartner says that, on average, a fully supported mobile workforce will require five times the number of help desk personnel for support.

Part of the task of the IT department will be to get everyone on board with these new technologies to ensure that everyone in the mobile communications loop can, in fact, communicate and access appropriate corporate services. This may mean that current business users of wireless services may have to give up their favored device and service in order to adopt the corporate standard. Also, as they have in the past with PC hardware and software, IT managers will have to deal with fast-changing technologies and new issues, such as telecom regulatory matters.

IT departments must also consider how widespread mobile use will impact their company's network management and overall performance. Indeed, with most IT budgets growing from year to year and with most of the new funding going to Internet initiatives and e-business, how will mobile/wireless technologies fit into your company's current IT infrastructure? At some point, IT department heads, working with corporate management, will have to decide how important these new and emerging technologies are to the company from a competitive point of view. How important is it, for example, for the company's sales force to be able to access real-time product pricing, availability, and service information while sitting in a customer's office?

Another issue is technical standards. As a company's mobile strategy develops and matures, a large percentage of employees will be required to use the same mobile platform, both hardware and software, and they must be synchronized with what already exists on their desktop PCs.

With employees working at different levels and in widely different functions— e.g., corporate management, public relations staff, traveling salespeople, each with their own specific mobile technology requirements—it is conceivable that IT department managers will have to appoint what amounts to a chief mobility officer to focus on the development and operation of the company's mobile telecom and computing activities.

An AFCOM survey taken in early 2001 shows that the advent of wireless applications is triggering significant changes to procurement plans. Some of the more dramatic examples are:

- Sixty-one percent of the survey's respondents say that their organizations need to purchase additional software to accommodate wireless technology.

■ Fourteen percent say that wireless will also cause them to increase purchases of storage-related solutions.

■ Nine percent believe the adoption of wireless solutions will drive up consulting budgets.

1.7 What is the Japanese government doing to advance its mobile IT activities?

The Japanese government has compiled a very ambitious "e-Japan Priority Policy Program" aimed at making Japan the world's most advanced IT nation within five years. It addresses a number of mobile technology-related issues, including the Internet and the need to assign new radio frequencies for high-speed wireless services.

■ The program is led by Japan's Information Technology Policy Office.

■ Impressively, Japan has established an ultra high-speed network infrastructure.

■ Japan hopes to significantly upgrade the skills of its own IT professionals.

Tell Me More

Led by the Japanese government's Information Technology Policy Office, the e-Japan Priority Policy Program consists of more than 200 government actions. The program is scheduled to get underway in 2001. Its key features include the introduction of new regulations and an incentive-based competition policy, the formation of a Telecom Conflict Resolution Committee, and expansion of the radio frequency spectrum to accommodate new, high-speed wireless network access. By 2002, Japan wants to standardize cryptographic technologies to ensure that its companies are using government-approved security systems in both their internal and mobile telecom and computer services. Plans also call for Japan to "more actively contribute" in the development of international standardization of telecom rules and specifications.

Another aspect of the program is to facilitate electronic commerce in Japan by revising regulations that hinder e-commerce, clarifying existing rules as they relate to e-commerce, and adopting legislation concerning electronic contracts and the protection of consumers.

In a related development aimed at promoting a national IT policy, Japan's Information Technology Policy Office says it plans to emulate and even exceed the skills of IT instructors and technical professionals in the United States. It hopes to accomplish this by 2003.

1.8 What is the Mobile Management Forum?

The Mobile Management Forum (MMF) is a U.S.-based organization dedicated to speeding the adoption of wireless and mobile solutions in business. It is part of The Open Group, a consortium of vendors committed to integrating new and emerging technologies into their businesses.

- MMF research will focus on several business-oriented technical issues.

Tell Me More

Co-founding members of the MMF include Argo Interactive, Boeing, Brand Communications, Compaq, Diversinet, hereUare Communications, Hewlett-Packard, Hitachi, IBM, JP Morgan, Motorola, NCR, NEC, Sun Microsystems, Symbian, and Synchrologic.

Research conducted by The Open Group will focus on several areas, including wireless devices and applications, data synchronization of mobile devices and networked data, coexistence of wireless local area networks, and merging personal area network technologies.

1.9 How does customer relationship management apply to mobile technologies?

Customer relationship management (CRM) started out as an information technology-driven method for businesses to generate sales leads and better to manage company contacts. Today, CRM is that and much more—providing companies with a new level of services ranging from developing sophisticated means of staying close to their customers to projecting how much revenue a customer or client might generate over an extended period of time. Increasingly, these concepts are now being applied to the mobile environment.

- A recent development is the mobile CRM (mCRM), which applies to mobile business/professional users.

- *Datamonitor* reports that the "real market" for mobile/wireless CMR is in the business-to-employee area.

- CRM vendors are now targeting the mobile "road warrior."

Tell Me More

As the old Pareto rule tells us, 80 percent of the revenue comes from 20 percent of the customers. Many companies are taking a much closer look at how to do a better job of retaining their customers. Increasingly, companies are developing techniques to more rapidly launch new products and services, identifying up-sell and cross-sell opportunities, and generally doing a better job of collecting and analyzing customer information.

A report on mCRM by *Datamonitor* suggests that the real market for mobile/wireless customer relationship management applications will be in the business-to-employee (B2E) area, in particular in developing and enhancing B2E sales applications. The pervasiveness of mobile devices, like cellular phones and PDAs, and the increasing bandwidth available to these devices, means that the mobile/wireless channel is one that businesses, and consequently CRM vendors, cannot afford to ignore. *Datamonitor* expects the global investment in mCRM in the B2E space to grow from $70 million in 2000 to $1.3 billion in 2005.

One of the most recent developments in CRM is applying its concepts to mCRM, and, by extension, to the business/professional mobile user.

Using mCRM techniques, companies can:

a. Select the information they want about their customers.

b. Develop comprehensive pictures of customers and their products and services.

c. Evaluate customers' near- and long-term requirements.

d. Make that information immediately available to people in the company who need it.

1.10 What companies have developed mobile CRM initiatives?

Several companies have announced plans to develop mobile customer-relationship management (mCRM) programs or applications. Increasingly, companies that develop these programs are looking at the mobile "road warrior" as a potential customer for its products and services.

Some specific examples include:

■ *PeopleSoft,* an e-business applications developer, now offers its CRM Mobile Sales for Wireless Applications Protocol (WAP) to give field sales personnel access to customer service data from any WAP-based cellular phone with PeopleSoft software. PeopleSoft also offers a service that enables field sales and service personnel to use a two-way pager to obtain data from anywhere. Mobile users can view and update data from the corporate database in real-time.

■ *Siebel Systems,* another specialist in e-business applications, and Sprint PCS are jointly marketing and selling nationwide access to Siebel's e-business products using the Sprint PCS Wireless Web for Business. Via the microbrowser used to access the Web on any Sprint PCS Internet-ready phone, business customers can have instant remote access to applications for reviewing and updating sales opportunities, information on products and services, and order status, and they can respond to service requests directly from customers.

■ *MyAlert,* a free wireless portal that connects mobile phones to the Internet, is using Broadbase Software's mCRM applications to target customers with relevant and personalized offers through the 500,000 alerts it issues per day to its more than one million customers. MyAlert users can register free by simply providing a user name and password to get personalized and time-critical information like stock quotes, travel information, special offers, or e-mail anywhere, anytime; they can also conduct mobile commerce transactions through their mobile phones. Users can choose what information they want. By incorporating its analytic software into the MyAlert system, Broadbase can identify and track customers' needs and behavior and target them with personalized advertisements and information.

■ *Remedy Corp.* has introduced Remedy Sales Continuum and Remedy Link for Palm handhelds to access corporate data stored in Remedy CRM and information technology service management (ITSM) applications. Mobile employees can now access and update corporate data via their Palm handhelds in the field. For example, field technicians can view and enter service-call information from the problem site. Field reps can carry the latest customer, product, pricing, and order status information, and they scan inventory information from remote locations.

■ *Motorola* is adopting Mobilize Web, developed by Mobilize, Inc., to distribute promotional and other literature through its newest handsets. The literature distribution feature of Mobilize Web enables users to e-mail or fax documents directly to customers using mobile phones, eliminating costly and time-consuming mailings and virtually ensuring that anyone receiving the literature will see it. Users can also order on-demand printing, binding, and courier services through print fulfillment partners, including NowDocs. This feature can also be used to place an order for pre-printed literature and promotional materials to be fulfilled at a printing center.

■ *Hoover's*, an online business information service, has introduced Hoover's Wireless, which allows people to tap into key content and service offerings remotely. Hoover's Online (www.hoovers.com) is now available from anywhere and from virtually any wireless device. Wireless device users can search for and retrieve information on approximately 17,000 public and private enterprises worldwide via Hoover's Wireless. Searches can be done on Hoover's Online by company name or ticker symbol to find company descriptions, locations, financial information, corporate officers, competitors, stock quotes, and company news.

1.11 Are wireless devices hazardous to your health?

Research on this subject has accumulated over the years, and several studies, including some very recent research, continue to frustrate wireless equipment manufacturers and consumers because of their generally mixed findings.

- Tests conducted by wireless equipment manufacturers and the industry's largest trade association indicate there is no health danger from using cellular phones.

- A Danish study found that cell phone users were no more likely to have cancer than the country's general population.

- A group of experts in the United Kingdom found that wireless phone use poses no health risk.

- A study by the American Health Foundation has found no relationship between using cellular phones and the risk of brain cancer.

However:

- Integrated Laboratory Systems in North Carolina found that radiation from wireless phones causes genetic changes in human blood cells under certain conditions.

Additional research is scheduled, focusing on people who were early subscribers to cellular phone service. In the meantime, wireless trade associations have made a number of recommendations about how to use cellular phones more safely, such as using an earphone attachment to keep the antenna away from your head.

Tell Me More

Tests conducted over a period of years by wireless equipment manufacturers, such as Motorola and Ericsson, have found no health danger to users of cellular phones. Similar negative results have been reported by a study group sponsored by the U.S.-based Cellular Telecommunications and Internet Association (CTIA).

One of the most recent studies—conducted by the Danish Cancer Society and the U.S.-based International Epidemiology Institute, and published in the February 2001 issue of the *Journal of the National Cancer Institute*—tested more than 420,000 Danish cellular phone users between 1982 and 1995. The study found cellphone users were no more likely to develop cancer than the general population of Denmark.

In May 2000, a group of experts in the United Kingdom reporting to the U.K. Government on issues related to the safety of wireless phones and antenna sites, found that the use of wireless phones poses no known health risk. However, the researchers said there should be further research to address specific scientific issues raised in the media and elsewhere, particularly fears about the use of wireless phones by children.

A study published in December 2000 by the American Health Foundation comparing 469 people with brain cancer with 422 healthy people found no relationship between the use of cellular phones and the risk of brain cancer. However, another study conducted in 2000 by the Integrated Laboratory Systems in North Carolina found that radiation from wireless phones causes genetic changes in human blood cells under certain conditions.

More research is scheduled, and since cancer usually develops over a period of years, some of the new studies will focus on people who were early subscribers to wireless services. Meanwhile, wireless industry trade associations recommend that cellular and PCS subscribers use earphones designed specifically for their cellular phones, or hands-free cradles when talking on their phones in their vehicles. By doing this, they are keeping the most critical radiation element in the phone, the antenna, away from their head.

1.12 What is data synchronization?

Synchronization is the process of uploading and downloading information from two or more databases—for example, moving the data in a handheld PDA to a desktop PC—so that each database is identical. It enables the synchronization of remote data and personal information across multiple networks, platforms, and devices.

- Synchronization is now possible through a variety of network platforms.

- SyncML is the common language for data synchronization for mobile devices.

- New software products, such as TrueSync, have been introduced that make it possible to enter data into a mobile device and then access that data from any SyncML-compliant device using Bluetooth technology.

- adAlive has installed wireless Internet access points at JFK International Airport.

Tell Me More

Until recently, mobile data synchronization among various wireless products has been very limited, with each product operating with different, often proprietary protocols, functioning only with a very small number of devices, systems and data types. These incompatible technologies made it difficult for developers, service providers, manufacturers, and users to extend the use of their mobile devices, restricting data access and limiting the mobility of the users.

SyncML, a consortium initiated by Ericsson, IBM, Lotus, Matsushita, Motorola, Nokia, Palm, Psion, and Starfish Software and now comprised of more than 500 supporting companies worldwide, has released the SyncML 1.0 specification providing synchronization for mobile devices.

SyncML is the common language for synchronizing all devices and applications over any network. SyncML leverages Extensible Markup Language (XML), making SyncML a future-proof platform. With SyncML, networked information can be synchronized with any mobile device, and mobile information can be synchronized with any networked applications. Using SyncML, any personal information—e-mail, calendars, to-do lists, contact information, and other personal data—will be consistent, accessible and up to date, no matter where the information is stored. In addition, SyncML enables synchronization over fixed networks, infrared, cable, or Bluetooth.

Starfish Software has already demonstrated the synchronization of calendar and address book data between Motorola's Timeport 270c mobile phone and Starfish's SyncML-enabled TrueSync server (also Microsoft Outlook 2000), using Bluetooth technology. TrueSync enables wireless-phone customers to enter personal information into a mobile device and then access that data from any SyncML-compliant device.

Another company, adAlive, has installed a network of Internet access-points at the American Airlines terminal in New York's JFK International Airport. With these free access points, users can download city guides and travel-related information. They can also synchronize Palm applications, such as the AvantGo mobile Internet service and Vindigo, and backup and update calendar and address book data. The system is expected to be installed at other airports, as well as in hotels and retail centers. Significantly, SyncML further strengthened its position as a universal data synchronization protocol when the Third Generation Partnership Project (3GPP), the standardization forum for 3G mobile systems, accepted SyncML as the protocol for future mobile data synchronization services. The agreement means that SyncML will replace the existing IrMC standard for network synchronization in 3GPP applications.

1.13 Can you use e-mail or access the Internet while on a commercial airline flight?

Currently, it is possible to make phone calls and send and receive e-mail on many commercial aircrafts. Full Internet access is not available on commercial flights, but it's coming.

- Broadband access for Web surfing and sending e-mail at T1 speeds could be available on some commercial flights by the end of 2001.

- Inmarsat, the international satellite organization, is developing a high-speed in-flight satellite network that is scheduled for service in 2004.

Tell Me More

Broadband access for surfing the Web and sending e-mail and other files at T1 speeds—1.5 megabits per second—could be available on some commercial flights as early as the end of 2001. In December 2000, Air

Canada became the first commercial airline to enable passengers to send and receive e-mail on their laptop computers while in flight. If ongoing in-flight tests prove successful, Air Canada will install the system throughout its fleet. Singapore Airlines transmitted an e-mail message while flying over the Pacific in April 2001, and now has the capability to plug passengers' laptop computers into in-seat telephone ports to send and receive e-mail and browse 30 Web sites. However, some in-flight communications systems are being designed to operate at lower transmission speeds and will have more limited access to e-mail messaging and the Web.

Singapore Airlines has also rolled out its Flight Status and Flight Alert mobile services to NTT DoCoMo's i-mode mobile phone subscribers, enabling the airline's customers to obtain information on request using PDAs, mobile phones, and PCs. But none of these airlines will have the same level of access to the full World Wide Web (WWW) that its customers are used to having on their office and home PCs, partly because of onboard server capacity issues, but also because billing systems are not fully in place for even the limited access services now available.

Boeing Commercial Information Systems has been working on a system that uses a very sophisticated antenna technology, which transmits and receives Internet data through two antennas mounted on the aircraft's fuselage. Passengers will have access to two jacks in the seat in front of them—one for use with a conventional modem in their laptop computer, the other a standard Ethernet connection like those in many offices. The Boeing system is designed to be installable in all major commercial aircraft.

Inmarsat, the international satellite organization, which already provides phone service in 78 percent of the world's long-haul commercial airliners, is developing a high-speed in-flight network that is based on a new, advanced series of satellites. These are not scheduled for service until 2004. Until then, Inmarsat will offer a service for airlines with e-mail and Web browsing at 64 kilobits per second.

Globalstar is also working with Network LLC, a joint venture of News Corp. and Rockwell Collins, to enable the In Flight Network to provide relatively low-cost broadband and e-mail, paging, and voice-over-IP services directly to passengers in existing commercial airline fleets. A prototype of the system has already been successfully tested in flights over parts of North America.

Under this venture, In Flight Network, Globalstar and Qualcomm will participate in the development of the system. Using a Globalstar satellite link, the system will initially operate at speeds in excess of 200 kilobits per second. When user demand increases, this data rate can be increased to more than 800 kbps, which is faster than most digital subscriber line (DSL) or cable modems. Full-scale deployment is planned for late 2001.

Despite all this activity, airlines still must convince the Federal Aviation Administration (FAA) that these systems will not interfere with any communications, navigation, or other electronic operations in commercial aircraft.

Another issue the FAA may be forced to revisit is the use of cellular phones on commercial flights. Several calls were made successfully by passengers during the September 11, 2001 terrorist attacks on the World Trade Center in New York City and on the Pentagon. Additional, extensive testing may be required to determine whether cellphones and other wireless devices interfere with aircraft operations, or with the terrestrial wireless infrastructure, before they are allowed to be used by passengers on commercial flights.

1.14 What laws, pending legislation, or regulations that affect mobile technologies does the United States have?

Public policy will play a critical role in the evolution of mobile information technologies. The Telecommunications Act of 1996 is the first significant legislation in the United States concerning the telecom industry since the Communications Act of 1934. It was primarily intended to create a more competitive environment by eliminating decades-old regulation and by opening up local markets to competition. However, the Telecom Act of 1996 did not anticipate the dramatic growth of mobile technologies and the Internet.

■ Congress is considering updating the Telecom Act of 1996.

■ A new advocacy group has been formed to promote the "promise" of the Telecom Act of 1996.

- New legislation will need to address the Internet, and privacy and security.

- Congress is working on a major piece of legislation, called the Internet Tax Freedom Act.

- Many critical issues in telecommunications require working with international legislative and regulatory bodies.

Tell Me More

Under pressure from trade associations, local telecom carriers, and state and local regulators, members of the U.S. Congress have been openly discussing the need to update or even completely rewrite the Telecommunications Act of 1996.

A new advocacy group called Voices for Choices—with Steve Ricchetti, a former deputy White House chief of staff for the Clinton Administration, as its co-chairman—was formed in February 2001 to promote the "promise" of the Telecom Act of 1996, and it plans to lobby for more choices in local phone services, improved service quality, and lower phone bills for both wireless and wireline services.

Issues to be addressed in any new legislation are likely to include industry consolidation, spectrum assignments and auctions, privacy and security, wireless network access, local exchange services, and competitive issues.

Important issues before the U.S. Congress and the FCC that would have some impact on the development of mobile technologies include Third Generation (3G), software-defined radio, mobile privacy, digital hearing aids, and Internet tax freedom.

Third Generation. Much of the debate here centers on the need for more spectrum (radio frequencies or airwaves) to ensure that advanced Third Generation (3G) wireless services can be deployed as envisioned by the telecommunications industry and the marketplace.

Wireless carriers favor a relaxation of a government-imposed spectrum cap, which, under current rules, gives them limited access to additional radio frequencies for 3G and other advanced services. Wireless carriers want a larger slice of the most desirable airwaves for 3G, which are currently being used by the military and other government agencies. These agencies do not want to give up any of their radio frequencies, or move to other frequencies, mainly because of the high cost and time required to deploy new equipment.

The Federal Communications Commission (FCC) and the National Telecommunications and Information Administration (NTIA) have submitted several reports on how to meet 3G spectrum needs. Currently, the FCC oversees and auctions radio spectrum for commercial services in the United States, whereas the NTIA is responsible for the airwaves used by the federal government and serves as the telecommunications policy advisor to the President.

In July 2001, federal regulators delayed indefinitely the planned September auction of airwaves that television broadcasters are supposed to vacate as they move to digital signals. The FCC was scheduled to sell the airwaves currently assigned to broadcasters occupying channels 60 to 69, even though they do not have to move off these frequencies until the end of 2006, or when the penetration rate of digital television in the United States reaches 85 percent, whichever comes later. Several members of Congress, meanwhile, have indicated that they plan to introduce legislation that would completely revamp how spectrum is allocated to commercial services—including wireless—and government agencies, and how government agencies would be compensated if they are required to move to new radio frequencies.

The Wireless Communications Association International (WCAI) represents fixed wireless services, such as wireless PBX, which is easier and cheaper to use than cellular when you are in your building or factory but away from your desk, and wireless local area networks (WLANs), which allow the sharing of data and resources, such as printers, without the need to physically connect each node. WLANs can operate in campus-type environments. WCAI is competing with 3G and other mobile wireless interests in that it wants the FCC to avoid displacing its member companies from current frequency assignments to make room for 3G services.

Software-Defined Radio (SDR). SDR is expected to become an important wireless technology in the future. Essentially, SDR allows users to download upgrades and software fixes to their mobile devices. For example, Sony announced in July 2001 that it would recall 1.1 million cellular phones, most of which were incompatible with the network because of software flaws. All of these phones will have to be returned to Sony or its service representatives for repair. With SDR technology this would not be necessary because the phones could be reconfigured through over-the-air software.

The FCC is playing an important role in the development of SDR in that it has written a set of proposals for implementing this emerging technology and is expected to formalize rules covering SDR some time late in 2001 or early 2002. These rules would allow, for the first time, wireless device manufacturers and service providers to make over-the-air software modifications (see Question 4.2).

Mobile Privacy. Privacy is a major issue and could result in efforts to develop new legislation to protect consumers. Some services—such as "push technology," which enables advertisers to send promotional messages to consumers' mobile devices whether they want them or not—are being tested and discussed at several industry and governmental levels. The Cellular Telecommunications and Internet Association (CTIA) has written voluntary guidelines that would allow consumers to "opt in" to wireless Internet services, such as advertising, and it will lobby other industry groups to support and help promote these guidelines.

Several trials have also been conducted to test consumer interest in mobile services that require them to share personal preference data for free services or discount coupons at, for example, local restaurants or retail stores. Companies are also eager to learn whether consumers would be willing to participate in online market surveys where their identities could be known to the market research organization. How consumers and the Government react to these types of services remains to be seen.

U.S. lawmakers are also considering legislation that would restrict marketers from tracking people and selling data on their movements without their permission. Congress wants consumers to be able to choose whether they want their location monitored through their mobile phones, pagers, or PDAs. A proposed law would make wireless service providers tell subscribers when they are tracking their location. Even if they agree to disclose this data, wireless phone users would be able to review the information and correct errors.

Digital Hearing Aids. The hearing impaired have been concerned for years that digital wireless devices will not be compatible with their hearing aids, and have pressed the FCC to establish rules to ensure that mobile technologies are available to them. The Wireless Access Coalition has asked the FCC to develop technical guidelines covering hearing aid-compatible mobile phones.

With an estimated 28 million people in the United States with some degree of hearing loss, several wireless service providers are promoting Short Messaging Service (SMS) and two-way wireless text messaging as an alternative to desktop computers and teletypewriter (TTY) phones currently used by the hearing impaired. Cincinnati Bell Wireless, Arch Wireless, and WebLink Wireless have developed marketing campaigns to attract deaf and hearing-impaired consumers to their wireless text-messaging services. Text messaging is already widely used among the hearing impaired in Europe, where SMS is much more popular than in the United States.

Internet Tax Freedom Act. Another concern in the United States is the Internet Tax Freedom Act. Passed in 1998, it imposed a three-year moratorium on new Internet taxation to give an advisory committee time to study international laws and tariffs, as well as federal, state, and local laws that might have any impact on Internet transactions or access. The advisory group handed down its recommendations to Congress in April 2000. They included:

- A five-year extension of the tax moratorium

- Elimination of sales tax on Internet access and the sales of digital products

- Implementation of a uniform act on sales tax simplification

- Elimination of what the industry and its trade associations perceive as excessive tax burdens on telecommunications service providers

Congress is also considering two bills related to the Internet Tax Freedom Act.

■ *HR 4462* would extend the Internet tax moratorium by five years to allow the states sufficient time to develop and implement a uniform sales-and-use tax system. If adequate simplification is enacted by twenty states, the bill would allow the states to collect taxes from out-of-state services. The bill also provides authorization and consent for states to enter into an Interstate Sales and Use Tax Compact for such purposes. The bill has been referred to the House Judiciary and Rules Committees.

■ *S.2775* would extend the current moratorium on Internet access taxes and eliminate excess tax burdens on telecommunications service providers for four years. It would also provide states with a mechanism by which to collect taxes that are legally owed on Internet sales and remote sales. The bill has been referred to the Senate Finance Committee where it must win approval before it is sent to the full Senate for consideration.

1.15 What is the role of the International Telecommunications Union?

The Geneva-based International Telecommunications Union (ITU) is an agency of the United Nations. Its most important role is to formulate international technical standards for telecom services and allocate spectrum for wireless services. Less formally, it also serves as a referee for private sector and international political and regulatory policy disputes in the global telecommunications community.

■ The ITU has more than 600 nation and private sector members.

■ The ITU will have a key role in the development of 3G mobile communications systems.

■ Most countries work aggressively to promote their own telecom agendas to the ITU.

Tell Me More

The ITU has 188 nation members and more than 450 private sector members, whose products and services are directly impacted by ITU decisions and who generally agree to abide by the rulings of the international organization.

One of its most critical roles in recent years has been to monitor and report on the development of 3G mobile communications, which is expected to support wideband wireless multimedia capabilities.

In March 1996, under the guidance of the ITU, the Europeans launched the Universal Mobile Telecommunications System (UMTS) forum to advance the 3G agenda. Since then, UMTS has moved aggressively to develop a set of proposals for 3G portable/mobile communication systems and services.

UMTS is being developed by the Third Generation Partnership Project (3GPP), an organization of several international telecommunications-standards bodies, including the European Telecommunications Standards Institute (ETSI). The ETSI, which is the European Community's telecom standards development body, has announced its decision to accept a single standard for UMTS. The Institute said that it made the choice based on a proposal submitted jointly by several of the world's leading telecom equipment manufacturers, including Alcatel, Bosch, Ericsson, Italtel, Motorola, Nokia, Siemens, and Sony.

Most countries, particularly the United States, Japan, and Korea, have worked over the years to speed up the ITU's technology evaluation process, often developing and promoting their own proposals for submission to the ITU for consideration of world standards.

A key element of the ITU's work is the World Radiocommunications Conference (WRC), an international forum for developing and regulating spectrum allocation and use and communication satellite orbits. The WRC meets every two years, usually in Geneva. But with so many nations involved and each with its own agenda, the meetings often take weeks or months of negotiation to resolve issues ranging from the allocation of radio frequencies for global services (for example, satellite communications) to the development of technical standards for global telecom services. The United States is represented in these meetings primarily by telecommunications and regulatory specialists from the

Federal Communications Commission and a corps of diplomats from the State Department.

Notes

1. Sources for the projections made in this section include Cahners In-State Group, Dataquest, Gartner Group, IDC Marketing and Advisory Services and Forecasts, Ovum Wireless Research, and The Yankee Group. The data was compiled by nSeconds, Inc.

Chapter 2

Mobile Internet and Data Services

2.1 How is the mobile Internet important to corporations?

As should be fairly obvious by now, the mobile Internet is the wireless version of the Internet, enabling anyone, anywhere to gain access to the World Wide Web (WWW). Many business organizations have taken a go-slow approach to adopting the mobile Internet into their operations.

- Access to corporate databases will be a key element in the development and success of the mobile Internet.

- New applications that embody both wireless hardware and Internet connectivity are rapidly emerging to address the needs of business users.

- Many businesses are concerned about the potential risks involved in rapidly integrating mobile technologies into their operations and, in fact, are not readily prepared to do so.

Tell Me More

Wireless device market penetration is high around the world and continues to grow. The growth rate in high-speed lines connecting homes and business to the Internet in the United States was 158 percent in 2000. Combining mobile technologies and the Internet should change the way everyone does business. Companies will now have quick and increasingly easy access to customers and prospects. Still, many business organizations have taken a go-slow approach to adopting the mobile Internet into their operations.

One of the more obvious advantages of the mobile Internet in the enterprise is access to corporate e-mail and databases (including business contacts, financial data, market research, and calendar information). Another advantage is advanced security features, usually with options that might include user authentication, encryption, physical security, and public key infrastructure (PKI) security (See Question 11.3). Message delivery confirmation to ensure completed transactions is also considered an important feature of many corporate mobile Internet systems.

Any browser-equipped mobile device should enable employees to send and receive e-mail, access an electronic bulletin board, and search the office directory. Additional down-the-road features will include accessing mobile customer relationship management (CRM) tools and sales force support, accessing procurement facilities and management reporting information, obtaining weather reports, making travel arrangements, and banking.

The benefits available to corporate mobile Internet users were identified by Accenture (formerly Andersen Consulting) in a Spring 2001 management report, "M-Commerce in Action." Among them were:

- Secure and controlled wireless access to a personalized selection of corporate information sources and applications

- Reduced time and location constraints associated with accessing corporate information technology applications

- Increased ability of mobile employees to interact

■ The ability to support faster decision-making based on real-time information.

As wireless devices and Internet connectivity proliferate, new applications will emerge to address the needs of the enterprise. However, instituting many of these features may take longer than some analysts have projected as many business organizations are taking a slow, even skeptical approach to fitting mobile Internet applications into their operations.

While consumers continue to look for convenience and many have been quick to add online purchases to their regular shopping experience. However, the benefits of m-commerce—that is, purchasing goods online via a portable, wireless device—is not entirely clear to many consumers. Also, given consumers' apathy toward using wireless data, and the difficulty some consumers have in navigating some of the more advanced features of their wireless devices, it may take longer than expected to match published market projections for this sector. At the same time, many businesses have expressed concern about the potential risks involved in adopting new technologies on any kind of scale. In fact, studies have indicated that few companies have developed a process to identify and manage their technology investment risk. Such risks would include system security and liability issues.

Nevertheless, many businesses are moving aggressively ahead with plans to use the mobile Internet to boost their competitive edge, and as a way to differentiate themselves from their competitors.

2.2 Why can't a Web-enabled device access every service that is already available on the Internet?

The Internet most people are familiar with is not the same as the mobile Internet. In fact, the mobile Internet represents a much smaller subset of data than the traditional Internet. Browsers—the software developed to move documents on the Web to your mobile phone, PDA, or computer—require sites to be specially coded with Handheld Device Markup Language (HDML) or Wireless Markup Language

(WML), and this has not been done across the broad spectrum of Internet sites. The result, obviously, is that many sites are not yet accessible to wireless users.

- Accessing the mobile Internet has been slow, expensive, and confusing.

- Several wireless Web services are available and more are emerging.

- Wireless Application Protocol (WAP) has been a major culprit in the slow development of the mobile Internet.

Tell Me More

To a large extent, getting information to a mobile phone has been a slow, expensive, and confusing process. With at least three different and competing digital wireless technical standards to choose from and more to come as wireless communications advances toward next-generation services, promoting the mobile Internet and other wireless data services has been a hard sell for network operators.

Most people using the mobile Internet today have signed on with a wireless Internet service provider, such as OmniSky, GoAmerica, or YadaYada, which deliver specially formatted Internet content. Several mobile Internet phone services, such as AT&T Digital PocketNet Service, Sprint PCS Wireless Web, Verizon Wireless Mobile Web, and Nextel Online, are being offered in more areas over time. Two-way paging services for accessing the mobile Web using Research In Motion's devices are SkyTel eLink and Go.Web.

The Wireless Application Protocol (WAP) that is designed to reconfigure Web pages into a mobile format so they can be read on cellular phones, PDAs, notebook/laptop computers, and other wireless devices has been a key issue in the slow development of the mobile Internet (See Question 3.1). WAP has simply not been up to the task.

The biggest rap on WAP is that it is too slow to be useful to most mobile users. Also, many subscribers believe that the screens on most mobile devices are too small and too difficult to read to make them useful as a business tool. Users of WAP-enabled mobile phones have also reported problems receiving Web-based forms, and receiving error messages such as "Web site not WAP-enabled." From a corporate cost standpoint, WAP phones add data service to the standard voice charges and carriers bill by the minute for Web access. Of course, there is also the cost of a mobile device (usually a phone or PDA) and the monthly subscription fee.

Nevertheless, the introduction of WAP version 2.0 by the WAP Forum with several new features, including the ability to recognize the size and characteristics of the mobile terminal screen, and the type of Web navigator being used, is expected to slowly but steadily boost the number of WAP users worldwide.

One thing that doesn't seem to change among Internet users, whether they are working on a desktop PC or accessing the Internet via a mobile device, is how they use the Internet. By far, according to most surveys, most people (about 70 percent) use the mobile Internet to access their e-mail. Research ranks second (just over 30 percent), and playing games third (about 25 percent).

2.3 What are the currently available and fast-emerging business applications on the mobile Internet?

New mobile Internet applications are evolving all the time. Currently, the most popular are personal information management services (PIM) and entertainment, such as games, but personal financial services and Internet browsing are gaining in user interest. Over the next few years, while PIM and entertainment (which increasingly will include video clips and music) will likely remain at or near the top of the list, location-based services are expected to become more popular.

Current and emerging applications usually fall into four categories. These include:

1. Corporate Applications

2. Telemetry

3. Field Service

4. Consumer Applications

Tell Me More

I. Corporate Applications

■ **Mobile Messaging** includes SMS for sending short text messages of up to 160 characters to mobile phones, voice mail, e-mail, and faxes.

  ■ Short Messaging Services (SMS)

  ■ E-mail

  ■ Unified Messaging

■ **Mobile Office** is used for accessing e-mail, the corporate intranet, Internet, corporate databases, and for downloading presentations and other corporate information and data.

  ■ Corporate e-mail

  ■ Intranet browsing

  ■ File transfer

■ **Corporate GroupWare** is used for accessing corporate information and personal business-related files.

  ■ Corporate information/news

  ■ Travel/directory service

  ■ Personal information management (PIM) synchronization

■ **Teleconferencing** is used for online audio, video and/or data conferencing from multiple locations, including sharing documents, spreadsheets, and other applications.

  ■ Collaborative working (networked meetings)

  ■ Telemedicine

2. Telemetry

■ **Remote Monitoring & Control** is used for wirelessly transmitting data from a remote site (inventory, sales, meter reading, photographic and video images, systems status, etc.).

- Vending machines

- Ticket machines

- Automatic metering

- Video surveillance

- Point-of-sale

- Parking and tolls

- Vehicle tracking

- Route guidance

- Alarm systems

- Health care

3. Field Service

- *Real-Time Business Process Support* includes two-way radio dispatch and monitoring services for truck and delivery fleets, as well as real-time sales and inventory data service.

- Dispatch

- Fleet management

- Emergency services

- Utilities

- Field service management

- Sales force/inventory management

- Preventive maintenance

4. Consumer Applications

- *Information/Entertainment* for instant news reports, sports results, and directory information.

- News and sports

- Financial

- Directory inquiries

- Yellow Pages

■ *Mobile Messaging* is used for short text messaging, voice mail, e-mail and faxes.

- Short Messaging Service (SMS)

- Internet e-mail

- Unified messaging

■ *Travel/Location* includes real-time traffic updates, in-vehicle navigation and location services, and calendar information.

- Traffic information

- Navigation services

- Location services

- Time tables

- Travel schedule updates

■ *M-Commerce* mainly is used for online mobile banking and other financial services as well as for online mobile shopping and ticketing.

- On-line banking

- Intelligent brokering

- Gaming/gambling

- Interactive shopping

- E-cash

- Music downloads

- Electronic ticketing

■ *Internet Access*

- Web browsing

- Portals

2.4 When will Web-based mobile technologies be widely available?

Expectations by industry analysts who track mobile technologies range all over the lot. With the development of new technical standards, it is most likely that products and services with higher-speed data transmission will become more widely available during 2002. However, more advanced, so-called Third Generation (3G) wireless products and services, with new, easy-to-navigate Internet access, which are discussed in detail in Chapter 12, are not expected to be available on any scale in the United States until at least 2003.

- The outlook is for more mobile devices than desktop PCs.

- Internet use continues to grow at a rapid pace, particularly in the United States.

- More than half the U.S. population logs onto the Internet every day.

- The shift to the mobile Web will require extensive education for new users.

Tell Me More

Just about everyone agrees that there will be more mobile handsets in use by the end of 2003 than desktop PCs connected to the Internet.

As an indication of the growth rate of new Internet subscribers in the United States, data filed with the Federal Communications Commission (FCC) by service providers shows that high-speed lines connecting homes and businesses to the Internet increased to 7.1 million in 2000, or 158 percent more than the previous year.

More than half of the U.S. adult population used the Internet in 2000, including some 16 million new users going online in the last six months of the year, according to a study by Pew Internet & American Life Project.

On the downside, few people, certainly few Americans, have demonstrated any pent-up demand for current-level wireless data services. Surveys have also indicated some concern among end users about the ease-of-use of handheld wireless devices with advanced features and small displays. This is expected to change with the introduction of higher-speed, more highly featured next-generation mobile devices.

Also, a study by Allied Business Intelligence found that as mobile phone use explodes throughout the United States, movement to the wireless Internet may involve an extensive education process to be successful, something that few manufacturers or carriers have been very good at and, in fact, are ill quipped to handle. Although many people are finding their mobile phones to be indispensable, not many are aware of the phone's wireless Internet capabilities, or have not made the effort to learn how to use them, according to the study.

2.5 What are wireless application service providers?

The primary duty of a wireless application service provider (WASP) is to acquire or develop appropriate application software for its corporate clients. Increasingly, however, WASP clients are looking for help in integrating their wireless applications with their existing IT systems.

- WASPs provide an expert source for applications software for business.

- WASPs often end up competing with their clients' internal IT departments.

- Using WASPs is expected to boost the number of mobile users by simplifying applications delivery.

- WASPs must stay abreast of new software developments.

Tell Me More

WASPs provide a variety of outsourced telecommunications and related administrative functions for companies of all sizes. Most often, these services include managing e-mail and other messaging applications, as well as document and image management and more broad-based functions, such as developing sales force automation software and customer relationship management software. In some cases, WASPs take on many basic administrative duties, including payroll, finance, and human resources.

Wireless applications present a very real and viable opportunity for ASPs. End users have strong ideas about the types of applications they expect to be available on a wireless solution. Not surprisingly, e-mail tops the list of these applications, but messaging and sales force automation applications are also rated highly.

From a business point of view, WASPs are often competing with a client's own IT department, or a management consulting firm. Also, a growing number of wireless network carriers worldwide have begun to offer application services, as well as some very specialized services, such as network surveillance, performance monitoring, help desk functions and security services.

Working in the fast-paced wireless technology area, to better advise their clients, WASPs should be keeping abreast of the latest software developments and know what suppliers can provide.

Strategy Analytics has identified four basic WASP customer segments:

- Commercial content providers/aggregators

- Customer-facing businesses

- Enterprises

- Wireless carriers/portals

The needs of these groups vary greatly, and no single approach suits every customer. According to Strategy Analytics, WASPs are thriving because of the uncertainty that now characterizes the fledging mobile Internet market.

2.6 What are wireless Internet service providers?

Like more traditional ISPs, which connect PCs to the Internet, Wireless Internet Services Providers (WISPs) have been established to enable mobile workers to connect to the Internet (at their office or home). Most of these, with access by modem and telephone line, are dial-up services. And like other telecom Internet service providers, wireless ISPs have identified a growing opportunity in developing applications for business customers who are looking for more effective ways to do their jobs while away from their offices.

- Business users have been the first to adopt wireless ISP services.

- Wireless ISPs are developing a growing number of business applications mostly for PDAs.

- U.S.-based WISPs are expanding into international markets.

Tell Me More

WISPs are attempting to give mobile professionals the same level of service they are currently receiving from their desktop PCs. WISP services usually include corporate e-mail and intranet access, e-business (including customer relationship management and sales force automation and collaboration), and financial services.

Most wireless ISPs have identified medium-sized and large businesses as the early adopters of wireless Internet services and are focusing their attention on that market, rather than on consumers.

For competitive reasons, a good deal of effort has gone into attempting to differentiate WISP services. To this end, a number of WISPs have formed relationships with data service providers, financial institutions, and others to help give them a leg up in the market.

With more than 47,000 subscribers at the end of 2000, GoAmerica provides several applications for the mobile worker that it calls its Go.Web service. Using PDAs—such as Microsoft's Pocket PC, Compaq's iPAQ, Hewlett-Packard's Jornada, Handspring's Visor, Palm PDAs— and Research In Motion's (RIM) two-way text messaging device, customers can access information on sales automation from a corporate database, along with competitive information, e-mail, and real-time two-way text messaging. Another GoAmerica feature is Law-On-The-Go, which gives lawyers wireless access to the Lexis.com research system from LEXIS Publishing, and the Shepard's Citation Service.

Financial services currently available to wireless subscribers via Go.Web include access to CSFBdirect Anywhere Wireless for tracking markets and monitoring personal portfolios from virtually any Web-enabled cellular phone, PDA, RIM pager, Windows-based laptop computer, or handheld PC.

In addition, GoAmerica provides several business-focused products and services across multiple handheld devices and laptops:

■ *Corporate e-mail and groupware applications* enable mobile workforces to view and interact in real-time with their e-mail, calendar, public and private folders, address books, memos, and tasks from virtually anywhere. This includes "push" e-mail alerts of new mail, which are automatically sent ("pushed") to employees' handheld devices and laptops.

■ *E-business*, including customer relationship management (CRM) and sales/field force automation, enables mobile sales and service representatives access to up-to-date customer information from the field.

■ *Financial services* for investment professionals (portfolio managers, analysts, equity and research sales, traders, and brokers) with real-time updates of all securities from the New York Stock Exchange, NASDAQ, American Stock Exchange, and the Options Pricing Resource Authority (OPRA). Additional data feeds and services include fixed income data, foreign exchange rates access to research on futures and options, and industry overviews.

■ *Intranet access* offers access to corporate data, as well as Web-based data and data stored in databases located on company servers.

■ *Enterprise security* incorporates over-the-air security for wireless transport and virtual private networks (VPNs) for corporations requiring a higher level of security.

With more than 34,000 subscribers at the end of 2000, Omnisky's Os Corporate Link allows access to corporate e-mail from behind a firewall. Systems have to use Microsoft Outlook-based PC and cellular digital packet data (CDPD) networks for sending digital data over the analog phone network.

YadaYada launched its own wireless ISP service early in 2001. It uses the CDPD network and connects through either a Handspring Visor, Palm V, or Vx PDA.

Another is Earthlink, whose Earthlink Everywhere provides wireless access to e-mail and the Internet from several wireless devices, including the BlackBerry text messaging device.

2.7 What "name brand" mobile data services are available today?

The wireless data market is currently defined by several organizations and service offerings.

- Circuit-switched data service is available over existing analog and digital cellular networks worldwide.

- Business users have several service options for high-speed wireless data service.

- One of the oldest of these services, formerly known as Ardis, has expanded its service features for business or professional applications.

- Mobitex, developed by Ericsson and Swedish Telecom, is available in twelve countries throughout the world, including the United States.

Tell Me More

These services, which transmit data (as opposed to voice) traffic, use primarily either circuit-switched or packet-switched networks. *Circuit-switching*, a network switching technique that establishes a dedicated and uninterrupted connection between the sender and receiver, is already available across existing analog and digital cellular networks worldwide. Circuit-switching is used in standard telephone service.

Packet-switched services, which send data in bundles of data called packets, are available over dedicated frequency bands through several wireless carriers. Packet-switched networks are gaining for many applications because the technology is used for communications over the Internet. Other standards (such as iDEN) are pushing into wireless enterprise applications.

Many businesses with high-volume wireless data network require-ments have turned to dedicated services such as Motient (whose data ser-vice was formerly known as Ardis) and BellSouth Wireless Data (formerly RAM Mobile Data), or cellular digital packet data (CDPD), which provides data services over existing analog systems.

In February 1992, BellSouth entered into a joint venture with RAM Broadcasting to form RAM Mobile Data US and RAM Mobile Data UK. In 1998, BellSouth purchased RAM Broadcasting's financial interest in RAM Mobile Data US and changed its named to BellSouth Wireless Data.

In January 1998, the American Mobile Satellite Corp. paid Motorola $100 million to acquire Ardis, then the largest two-way data network in the United States. Covering some 425 cities, Ardis was used primarily by businesses that operated fleets of vehicles, and by government agen-cies, to send and receive data to and from drivers on the road. This included routing changes, customer contact information, and directions between deliver stops.

Motient, with approximately 206,000 subscribers at the end of 2000, has expanded its two-way network to include a wireless e-mail service designed to enable mobile workers to, for example, conduct sales transactions, as well as a satellite communications service for tele-phone, data, and fax connectivity. Motient is also providing Palm V users with a dash-mounted cradle that provides a constant connection to its wireless data network, and automatically alerts users to incoming mes-sages. Motient also offers its subscribers the use of Melard Technologies' Sidearm handheld computer, a rugged unit that runs Microsoft's Win-dows CE operating system.

BellSouth has based its wireless data service on Mobitex technol-ogy, a land-based, packet-switched radio system developed by Ericsson and Swedish Telecom. Mobitex enables two-way wireless data commu-nications and can be connected to other existing data networks. It is also designed to provide in-building coverage in major markets. With the merger of BellSouth and SBC Communications, the data service is now part of Cingular Interactive.

Outside of the United States, Mobitex technology is available from eleven national network operators in eleven countries throughout Europe, Asia, and South America. These include:

CANADA
Cantel Data

SOUTH AMERICA
Chile (CTC Communications Moviles S.A.)

EUROPE
Belgium (RAM Mobile Data Belgium)

Finland (Telecom Finland)

Netherlands (RAM Mobile Data Netherlands)

Norway (Tele-Mobile)

Poland (Bankowe Przedsiebiorstwo Telekomunikacyjne)

Sweden (Telia Mobitel)

United Kingdom (RAM Mobile Data)

ASIA/PACIFIC
Australia (United Wireless)

Singapore (ST Mobile Data)

Cellular digital packet data (CDPD) service was started in the United States in 1994 and has been deployed in many other countries. CDPD uses the radio channels in the cellular network to send bursts of data (or characters) in what are known as packets. This is done when the channels are not being used for voice transmissions. The data sent is then assembled by a packet assembler/disassembler, which can receive the packets and disassemble them into a format that can be handled by the mobile phone or other wireless device.

Since CDPD has access to so many cellular base stations, it offers fairly high quality signal coverage. However, some carriers do not offer

CDPD throughout their coverage areas because of the additional cost of providing the service. As a result, CDPD covers only an estimated 65 percent of the major metropolitan areas of the United States. For identification purposes, CDPD, or "packet data-ready" devices such as laptop computers, usually carry the Mobile End Station (MES) designation.

The all-digital personal communications services (PCS) in the United States and Nextel Communications also offer wireless data for business users.

Chapter 3

Software and Protocols

3.1 What is the Wireless Application Protocol?

Wireless Application Protocol (WAP) is a technology standard that enables applications to work over digital wireless networks. The protocol is designed to simplify how mobile device users access e-mail and voice mail, send and receive faxes, as well as use special interest features, such as trading stocks and playing games.

- WAP provides consistent content formats for delivering Internet- and intranet-based information and services to digital mobile phones and other wireless devices.

- WAP is a global open standard.

- WAP has been slow to gain wide acceptance because of slow connection speeds and dearth of applications.

- Improvements in WAP technology and security features are expected to vastly enhance its acceptance.

■ Ease-of-use should improve with new developments in the mobile infrastructure.

Tell Me More

WAP supports most wireless network standards, including CDMA, GSM, PDC, PHS, TDMA, FLEX, DECT, and Mobitex, as well as wireless operating systems like EPOC. WAP devices understand the Wireless Markup Language (WML) that is optimized for the small screens of mobile wireless devices. WAP also supports WMLScript scripting language.

WAP is a global open standard, which means that it is a free and nonproprietary system for wireless communications. As the wireless communications industry has already demonstrated with the adoption of a number of digital transmission standards (GSM, CDMA, TDMA, and others), the use of proprietary technical standards can lead to highly fragmented markets.

WAP is supported by a large number of industry suppliers. However, WAP is not without its detractors. Users have complained from the time that WAP was initially available that WAP's data transfer rate of 9.6 kilobits per second is too slow, particularly in networks using GSM technology where delays of up to 45 seconds to establish a wireless Internet connection have not been unusual. Detractors also point out that promised applications (such as finding local travel information) either continue to be unavailable to many users or are outdated in terms of their usefulness. Indeed, one industry columnist suggested that WAP should stand for "What A Pain."

Another common complaint is that the screens in WAP-enabled portable devices are too small to work with any useful text-driven applications. In fact, the WAP protocol is specifically formatted for small screens, such as those used in cellular phones and personal digital assistants. As a result, surveys of people with WAP-based devices indicate that they are using the WAP service infrequently.

In WAP's defense, the network infrastructures that can deliver Internet services to cell phones and other wireless devices are not in place. Also, security issues are a concern, particularly among potential business users of WAP applications. Another more common issue is a lack of understanding among users about what WAP-based devices can do.

On the upside, a new version of WAP is in development, and thousands of software companies have signed on to create products under the specifications of the upgraded version of the protocol. Features in this new version should help improve the technology and security in WAP. It should also become easier to use WAP once mobile connectivity is improved at the infrastructure level and once each new generation of wireless device is introduced with new data-rich features.

3.2 Will WAP work with XHTML?

Although HyperText Markup Language (HTML), the basic programming language of the Web, is defined for all application environments, a Wireless Markup Language (WML) has been developed that uses the Extensible Markup Language (XML); it is "extensible" in that it enables software developers to customize the language to their own data interchange needs. Significantly, XML adds to the capabilities of HTML by recognizing numbers and text, enabling this information to be shared between applications. WML is specifically optimized for wireless devices and networks.

Nokia, Motorola, Ericsson, Siemens and several wireless service providers, Web portals, and content providers have expressed their support for WAP/Web convergence. XHTML is the language that will be used to create all content for mobile and fixed wireless communications.

- Several mobile service providers are on board with XHTML-based services.

- Style sheets available with XHTML will add a custom content element for different handsets.

Tell Me More

In addition to the mobile handset manufacturers, a number of mobile service providers have announced their support for XHTML-based services. These include Orange, Radiolinja, Sonerea, the Vodafone Group,

Telenor, Netcom, T-mobil, the Telecom Italia Group, RadioMobil, and EuroTel Praha.

In addition to handset manufacturers and wireless carriers, several other companies also plan to launch XHTML services, application technology, and content creation tools. These include AOL, CNN, Sabre, Macromedia, Adobe, Oracle, and others.

One of the important elements in XHTML is the cascading style sheets that offer significant advances to how content is presented to the user. The style sheets will make it possible to easily tailor content specifically for different handsets and offer many of the elements necessary to create a graphical user interface (GUI) for services.

3.3 What is Java?

Java is a programming language developed by Sun Microsystems. It works on a variety of computer platforms ranging from supercomputers to desktops (PCs, Macintosh, and network computers) and mobile devices, including Internet-enabled handheld phones. With Java, mobile subscribers can upgrade their devices by downloading applications from the network.

Java software running on servers in large companies monitors transactions and links data from existing computer systems. Increasingly, companies are using Java software on their internal Web sites to streamline communications and the flow of information between departments, suppliers, and customers.

Java is incorporated into all major Web browsers and is beginning to show up in mobile phones, smart cards, and other devices. Java programs run on different kinds of systems through the Java virtual machine—a kind of translator that turns general Java platform instructions into tailored commands that make devices do their work.

- An industry survey indicates that there is a heavier concentration of Java users among wireless developers than in the general development population.

- Java can be delivered via a network or installed by more traditional media, such as CD-ROM.

- Java also works with mobile phones to display personalized information and end-to-end mobile Internet services.

- Several mobile phone vendors are currently shipping products based on Java technology.

- Java technologies offer several benefits to software and hardware developers and designers, and to consumers.

- Sun Microsystems and Openwave Systems have created a wireless developers program to support both Java and the Wireless Applications Protocol (WAP).

Tell Me More

A survey in March 2001 by Evans Data Corp. indicates that wireless developers will target Java and the Java2 Platform Micro Edition (J2ME) platforms in their application development. Almost a third of the developers interviewed by Evans Data said they have focused on Java and J2ME. The survey also revealed a heavier concentration of Java users among wireless developers than in the general development population.

J2ME is designed with the memory and processor limitations of small electronic devices, such as cellphones and personal digital assistants.

Java is typically delivered over a network. It can also be installed on computers from traditional media such as CD-ROMs. The same program or software component can run on a variety of computers and devices.

Java software also works in mobile phones with PersonalJava or EmbeddedJava. The software is built into the phone, or delivered in real time via a wireless connection. Applications include stock quotes, calendars, and address books. A screen display engine provides the visible interface on the phone and interacts with the Java virtual machine, which runs the software after doing security checks. Often, the Java virtual machine is integrated directly into the phone's real-time operating system, which provides device-specific support for actual operations.

Several mobile device vendors—including Motorola, Nokia, Siemens, Research In Motion, Sony, NEC, Matsushita/Panasonic, Mitsubishi, Fujitsu, Symbian, SmartTone, Far EasTone, Telefonica, Nextel, and One2One—have begun to ship mobile handsets and services based on Java technology.

These companies and others will use the Mobile Information Device Profile (MIDP) profile in their next generation devices. The MIDP is a set of open J2ME-based technologies specifically developed for the wireless platform by an expert group using the Java Community Process program.

For consumers, J2ME technology-enabled interactive services are the next step beyond today's text-based, static content. Java software supports easy-to-use graphical interactive services for wireless devices. With J2ME technology-enabled phones and other wireless devices, users can download new services for use while connected interactively or disconnected from the network.

Nextel's i85s and i50sx, both manufactured by Motorola, come pre-loaded with several Java applications, including specialized business calculators and an expense pad. As more J2ME-enabled applications are developed, Nextel customers will be able to download these applications onto their phones from the nextel.com website. Like all new Nextel phones, the i85s is Internet-ready.

Based on the J2ME, the MIDP enables highly differentiated interactive products and services. These include:

- Dynamically-generated, personalized stock quotes that can display graphs and give purchase and/or sell alerts for specific stocks using the wireless network

- Real-time, location-specific weather reports that display periodic forecast updates

- Real time, location-specific traffic reports that update local traffic conditions and supply alternative highway routes

- Games that can be downloaded and played offline by individual users

Java technologies also provide several benefits to wireless network services:

- Applications are loaded on demand. The user can choose to download applications on an as-needed basis rather than buying a device with applications pre-installed by the device manufacturer.

This protects the consumer's wireless device investment and allows carriers to enhance and expand their service offerings.

- Java technologies come with libraries that allow an applications developer to build a more intuitive graphic user interface (GUI). This enables service providers to offer personalized and more compelling applications and services.

- Java allows more intelligent use of network bandwidth because applications are downloaded onto the device and run locally. The network is only tapped when data is needed from the server.

- Java technology provides cross platform and multiple device support. J2ME and MIDP technologies can run the same application on any supported system type. This is a key feature for most users because there are so many different combinations of operating systems currently in use.

- Java on the wireless device reaches across multiple device types and across system platforms. Service providers can offer devices from multiple manufacturers without having to establish separate support for each.

In early 2001, Sun Microsystems and Openwave Systems (formerly Phone.com and Software.com) created a wireless developers program to support both Java and Wireless Application Protocol (WAP), which are complementary platforms. Sun Microsystems and Openwave will provide standardized access across mobile devices, while J2ME provides the WAP with additional security and functionality. J2ME will also make it easier to deliver dynamic content, such as personalized stock quotes with accompanying graphics.

3.4 What is Linux?

Linux is a royalty-free, nonproprietary computer operating system (OS)—a software program that manages the flow of information into and out of a computer processor (usually a chip or set of chips). It is based on another operating system, UNIX, which is widely used in large business organizations and by engineers for running high-traffic data processing operations and telephone systems.

- One advantage of Linux is that it can support product prototyping.

- Interest in Linux has grown because it is an ideal OS for systems with a limited memory capacity.

- Wireless applications written in Linux are outpacing other development applications, according to a mid-2000 survey by Evans Data Corp.

- A Korean firm has developed the first Linux mobile phone.

Tell Me More

One of the advantages of Linux is that it can simplify the process of prototyping and duplicating applications in new designs. It also includes a variety of networking options, giving mobile device manufacturers a choice of user interfaces. In addition, as a UNIX-based system, it can be used by many people at the same time. It is a very common OS for servers on the Internet.

Interest in Linux has grown dramatically among wireless application developers, mainly because its simplified process is ideal for products with limited memory capacity, such as cellular phones and other wireless devices. Linux is also popular with corporate IT departments because it can run full-blown office applications (such as accessing company data) rather than more limited portable versions on mobile devices.

Compaq developed the first prototype handheld device using the Linux OS in 1999. Called the Itsy, it was apparently never sold, but was simply meant to demonstrate that Linux can be modified for use in portable, low-power wireless devices and would support such applications as voice recognition.

On the downside, the rollout of new Linux-based mobile devices has been slow, partly because the development cost of Linux products has been high. Wireless device manufacturers have also been slow to commit to adopting Linux in their designs because the Linux community is required to declare any changes to the design of the Linux operating system kernel. This means that software developers and designers must share their intellectual property rights with other Linux developers, something that many of them are reluctant to do. A study in the summer of 2000 by the market research group, Evans Data Corp., found that only 20 percent of the developers surveyed were writing applications for mobile devices; however, this number reflected more than a 50 percent increase over Evans Data's spring 2000 survey. Significantly, Evans Data reported that wireless applications showed the largest increase in Linux use compared to applications for more traditional internal corporate use, e-commerce, and Web portals.

Meanwhile, Palm Technology has unveiled a Linux-based mobile phone, and IBM researchers are running Linux on a "smart" wristwatch as a demonstration of the viability of the operating system across all types of product platforms. Designed to communicate wirelessly with personal computers, cellular phones, and other wireless-enabled devices, the watch can display condensed e-mail messages and directly receive pager-like messages. Future enhancements of the watch, according to IBM, will include a high-resolution display and applications that will allow the watch to be used as an access device for various Internet-based services, such as up-to-the-minute weather reports, traffic conditions, and stock market and sports results. Of course, even though Linux is "free," software developers must still write (and eventually market) applications that will run on mobile devices.

3.5 What is IPv6?

IPv6, or Internet Protocol version 6, is the next generation protocol for the Internet. The Internet Engineering Task Force (IETF), the body that oversees the Internet, is developing IPv6 to replace IPv4, which has been around for about twenty years. (Work on an interim version that followed IPv4, known as ST, never got past the experimental stage, so there never was an IPv5.)

- An anticipated shortage of Internet addresses is a key reason for the development of IPv6.

- The development of IPv6 will accommodate the rapid growth of Web-enabled mobile devices.

- The first successful field trial of IPv6 was conducted in Hong Kong.

- IPv4 and IPv6 will co-exist for several years, but IPv6 will eventually replace IPv4.

Tell Me More

The key reason for upgrading the Internet Protocol (IP) is concern over the growing demand for Internet addresses, or routing numbers, particularly with the profusion of Web-enabled cellular phones and PDAs, and the introduction of new Internet-enabled mobile devices. More than half of the Internet connection points have already been assigned, and with two to three billion wireless device users anticipated globally in the next few years—a growing percentage of them Internet-enabled—there is simply not enough address space at the moment to support the system. Theoretically, IPv6 can support more than four billion Internet addresses, more than enough to cover the anticipated growth in the Internet worldwide.

Work on IPv6 has been underway for more than ten years. The core specifications for IPv6 became an IETF draft standard in 1998 and, although some changes are likely, they will not be major. Equipment manufacturers have only recently begun to support IPv6, mainly because migrating to the new, upgraded standard is costly and because of some perceived shortcomings in the standard itself.

Ericsson, BT Wireless, and SmarTone in Hong Kong conducted the first successful end-to-end demonstration of IPv6 in a mobile network toward the end of 2000. The SmarTone trial was built on Ericsson's network-enabling IPv6 systems, in conjunction with BT Wireless' R&D efforts. Partly as a result of this trial, a number of experimental IPv6 networks are in operation.

Major network infrastructure vendors, such as Cisco, plan to add IPv6 into their fixed Internet products. Nokia has already developed several products that incorporate IPv6, and plans to begin shipping IPv6-

enabled equipment by the end of 2001, and for Third Generation (3G) infrastructure wireless systems by 2002.

IPv4 and IPv6 are expected to coexist for several years, but IPv6 will eventually replace IPv4. However, shifting from IPv4 to IPv6 will not be easy. It requires the translation of IPv4 addresses into IPv6 address and vice versa. Also, many of the computer terminals used to access today's Internet do not have their own unique Internet address. Instead, they are assigned temporary addresses that are free for use elsewhere once an Internet session has ended.

Chapter 4

Software-Defined Radio

4.1 What is software-defined radio?

Software-defined radio (SDR) is a rapidly evolving technology that enables users to operate over virtually any wireless transmission standard. In other words, SDR-based phones or other wireless devices can function as multimode (analog or digital) and multiband (in virtually any radio frequency) devices. As the technology progresses, SDRs are expected to become almost totally software based. The operation of the radios will be performed in high-speed digital signal processors (DSPs), which translate incoming signals—such as voice impulses—into digital bits for controlling the various functions of the device.

- Through SDR, wireless networks can switch among different digital access technologies and add new services through software changes.

- SDR-enabled devices can be programmed remotely to reconfigure the requirements of the equipment.

- SDR gives end users flexibility in the choice of media content.

- The SDR Forum is dedicated to promoting the development, deployment, and use of open computer and telecommunications architectures for advanced wireless systems.

- SDR use is expected to grow rapidly over the next several years.

Tell Me More

SDR can operate across a range of voice and data services and can adapt to new voice and data services as they are developed and deployed. As a result, SDR is considered an enabling technology that is applicable to a wide range of applications within the wireless industry. SDR concepts are aimed at effectively integrating applications to work over any wireless access technology.

At the moment, mobile communications services are characterized by the use of mobile devices with competing and often incompatible technical standards, and operating in different radio frequencies. This trend is expected to continue into the next generation global standard for mobile devices. SDR can help alleviate some of these technical issues.

SDR-enabled devices can be dynamically programmed in software to reconfigure the characteristics of the equipment. In other words, an SDR-based device can be modified to perform different and unique functions that were not part of the device originally. Users have the benefit of a single product on which new features can be added. SDR concepts also permit network operators to differentiate their service offerings without having to support a wide variety of handheld device models.

SDR can enhance network flexibility by enabling wireless network operators to change digital network technologies and add new services primarily through software changes. Downloading software remotely via wireless transmission provides some obvious efficiencies for business users, from implementing software upgrades to fixing bugs. SDR also gives end users greater flexibility in the choice of programming content. Using SDR, manufacturers can consolidate their product platforms and reduce the design and manufacturing resources needed to accommodate the rapid growth of different digital cellular technical standards used around the world.

A November 1998 study by the SDR Forum, an international industry association dedicated to supporting the development and deployment of flexible architectures in advanced wireless systems, suggests that SDR may slowly gain acceptance as a wireless appliance or network standard. For the moment, it is still viewed as a design element to be incorporated into a future standard or standards. According to the study, the growth and development of SDR concepts will depend on how quickly it can penetrate into both mobile phones and the PDA/handheld PC markets.

4.2 How are SDR devices being used?

SDR is already employed in some cellular and Personal Communications Service (PCS) central radio transmitters/receivers (also known as a base station or cell site), as well as in military and aerospace equipment.

- SDR is expected to be used extensively in handheld terminals, such as cellular phones and PDAs.

- Although SDR concepts and techniques are in use right now, SDR has not gained wide acceptance as yet.

Tell Me More

So far, manufacturers have exploited SDR mainly to reduce the number of different product platforms that they must develop and support, and to enable new product designs and developments that can incorporate new features.

4.3 What is the status of federal regulations for SDR?

The Federal Communications Commission (FCC) began to take a serious look at SDR early in 2000, when it became convinced that SDR technology was a way to create more efficient radio frequency spectrum and help ease the process of allocating frequencies to wireless carriers and other service providers.

■ The FCC has prepared a formal proposal that would clarify the SDR under current Commission regulations.

■ The goal of the FCC is to redefine SDR as a new class of radio equipment.

Tell Me More

To formalize its action on SDR, the FCC prepared a Notice of Proposed Rulemaking (NPRM) on SDR to clarify that the technology is permitted under the current FCC rules. The FCC is also launching an effort to reduce the regulatory burden of re-certifying SDR radios (a process that ensures they meet all FCC technical specifications), and re-labeling SDR-compliant equipment, indicating that it complies with all appropriate FCC regulatory requirements.

But FCC rules, which long preceded the invention of SDR technology, have specifically prohibited changes to mobile radios once they have been sold. Technically, this would be enough to threaten a mobile device equipped with SDR from receiving FCC certification, without which the equipment would not be allowed to operate legally. The FCC is attempting to get around these long-standing rules by defining SDR-compliant radios as a new class of equipment. The FCC proposal would therefore permit equipment manufacturers to make changes in the frequency, power, and modulation of their radios without being required to file a new equipment authorization application with the Commission.

4.4 Are other industry groups addressing SDR-related issues?

The SDR Forum and other groups are banding together to address SDR issues.

■ The SDR Forum has established formal liaison activities with other industry groups.

■ One of the most important issues of interest to these groups is security.

Tell Me More

The SDR Forum, the lead international group promoting SDR development and applications, has established formal liaison activities with other industry groups, such as the 3G Partnership Project (3GPP), Mobile Station Application Execution Environment (MExE) Working Group, and the Wireless Application Protocol (WAP) Forum to address issues of related interest.

One of the most important of these issues is security. Although it is subject to ongoing study, electronic encryption techniques used in SDR have already been assessed by the MexE and WAP forums and have passed muster in terms of their acceptability for use in mobile electronic commerce applications.

4.5 When will SDR take off?

SDR will become more widely used starting in 2002.

- Next-generation wireless systems will help the increase of SDR adoption.

Tell Me More

The SDR Forum expects to see increased commercial, civil, and military use of SDR beginning in 2002, driven by the development of next-generation commercial wireless systems and a requirement for mobile communications systems that interoperate between United States and foreign military services.

It is expected that by 2005, SDR will be widely adopted as a core technology platform by many manufacturers of professional and consumer level wireless devices.

Chapter 5

Messaging Services

5.1 What is instant messaging?

Instant messaging (IM) enables people to carry on one or more real-time conversations in text windows that appear on a user's computer or mobile communications device screen. The text appears virtually simultaneously on the screens of one or more devices, making it more informal and conversational than traditional e-mail.

Because it is easy to use and efficient, instant messaging is very popular for international communications between business associates and friends, and those with hearing and speech disabilities.

- Instant messaging has gained popularity among business users because of its utility.

- The ability to exchange instant messages with someone who has a different Internet service is a recent development.

- A key feature of instant messaging is a buddy list for easily communicating with people on a regular basis.

■ The Federal Communications Commission has required AOL to make its system compatible other services.

■ Market studies indicate that the number of Americans who use instant messaging more than doubled from 1998 to 2000.

Tell Me More

Instant messaging has become very popular with business users who can, for example, conduct a "conversation" with a secretary or colleague while sitting in a meeting or at a conference. Users can respond immediately (or instantly) to messages received on a growing number of IM-capable devices. If necessary, this can be done in a surreptitious manner. In practice, the only difference between instant messaging and a voice conversation is that IM is being conducted in a text format, making responses generally shorter and more to the point.

Instant messaging is a proprietary technology (that is, owned and operated by a specific vendor) and until recently, it was impossible to exchange instant messages with anyone using a different Internet service. For example, Microsoft, Yahoo, AT&T, and ExciteAtHome users could not communicate "instantly" with America Online subscribers.

Attempts by many Internet services to make all instant messaging services compatible was challenged by AOL, which operates the two leading messaging services—ICQ and AIM—with more than 140 million users. A key feature of AOL's instant messaging service is the buddy list, which allows users to create a list of people they want to communicate with on a regular basis. It also allows users to see if anyone from their "buddies list" is online at any particular time.

AOL's proprietary grip on instant messaging was loosened, however, when the Federal Communications Commission made instant messaging compatibility a condition of its approval of AOL's merger with Time Warner. Under FCC orders, AOL was required to make its system compatible with the instant messaging system of at least two other services. IBM has also been pushing into the wireless IM arena with its Sametime Everyplace 1.0 software for users of Lotus Notes. (IBM is considered an important factor in the growth of IM because of its penetration and influence in IT departments, and because Lotus Notes has 80 million users.)

Most market studies indicate that the number of Americans who use instant messaging more than doubled from 1998 to 2000, from about 16 million to more than 33 million. Also, nearly three out of four online teenagers use instant messaging, according to the Pew Internet & American Life Project, a research group, whose survey indicates that they not only communicate with each other, but also with their teachers about schoolwork.

Clearly, much of the growing popularity in instant messaging is due to its ease of use and relatively low cost, which is why some studies indicate that IM will continue to gain in use among business professionals.

5.2 What is unified messaging?

Unified messaging combines voice mail, e-mail, and faxes into a unified system that can be stored and accessed from either a mobile phone or a PC. Introduced in 1998, it is achieving some penetration in smaller companies. In the future, larger companies with a high percentage of mobile workers will likely adopt the technology.

- Lucent Technologies provides its own unified messaging service.

- Several options are open to business users who want to use unified messaging services.

- There are also several suppliers of equipment for unified messaging.

Tell Me More

In 1999, Lucent Technologies entered the unified messaging market with a solution based on Microsoft Exchange and its own Unified Messenger system.

Options for business users include using a company's own technology through its existing in-house telecommunications equipment (usually referred to as customer premises equipment, or CPE), or by subscribing to a unified messaging service through a telecom service provider, which could be a landline carrier, wireless carrier, or an Internet service provider (ISP). Verizon Wireless, for example, provides a unified messaging service. Companies that provide unified messaging equipment include Active Voice and AVT. Companies that provide free basic unified messaging service include Yahoo!, Onebox, eFax, and MessageClick.

According to Ovum, which specializes in market research in telecommunications, the market potential for unified messaging remains unclear because of the uncertain levels of acceptance and growth of the wireless Internet and other free messaging services.

5.3 What is Multimedia Message Service?

Multimedia Message Service (MMS) is the next generation in mobile-to-mobile messaging after instant messaging. MMS can transmit messages containing text photos and audio and video clips via Wireless Application Protocol (WAP)-enabled mobile devices, including cellphones and PDAs.

- MMS traffic will create a new revenue stream for network operators.

- Technical specifications for MMS were written by the Third Generation Partnership Project (3GPP).

- Ericsson has announced the first MMS-equipped phone.

Tell Me More

MMS will create an essentially new revenue stream for network operators because it will generate more airtime use—actual time spent sending data over a cellular phone or other wireless device. Operators also anticipate that the new services will earn additional revenue via wireless advertising on the service.

In addition to sending messages between mobile devices, it is possible to send e-mail messages from a mobile device using MMS to an Internet e-mail box, and eventually users will be able to send e-mail to a mobile device.

Technical specifications have been developed by the Third Generation Partnership Project (3GPP), the global body dedicated to the development of 3G specifications.

Ericsson has announced the first mobile phone with MMS, the T68, available toward the end of 2001. It also features a color display, digital imaging, and built-in Bluetooth technology, and it supports General Packet Radio Service (GPRS), the emerging, high-speed upgrade (around 170 kilobits per second) for the digital Global System for Mobile Communications (GSM) technology standard.

5.4 What is Short Messaging Service?

Short Messaging Service (SMS) enables Web-enabled cellular phone users to send messages of up to 160 characters at a time by typing them on the keyboard of a phone or SMS-capable pager. Much more popular in Europe and Japan than the United States, SMS operates over a signaling or control channel that allows messages to be exchanged during an ongoing communications session.

- Most new SMS devices operate two-way.

- Sending SMS messages outside the cellular network requires using the Internet.

- SMS devices cannot exchange messages with devices attached to networks using different technical standards.

- SMS is much more popular in Europe than in the United States.

Tell Me More

When sending an SMS message within the local network, all you need is a telephone number. Sending a message outside the network requires using an e-mail address, which means that it is sent through the Internet rather than over the cellular network. Some people receive stock quotes and short daily features, such as their horoscopes and jokes, via SMS without realizing this is how the information is being transmitted.

One problem with SMS is that it is not compatible across wireless networks that use different technical standards. Europe, for example, has a single technical standard (Global System for Mobile Communications, or GSM) for digital cellular, while the United States operates mainly on different standards (namely CDMA and TDMA, described earlier). SMS also seems to be a cultural issue in that it is generally more popular in Europe than in the United States where people prefer to talk to each other rather than send even short text messages. Finland, for example, where nearly 80 percent of the country's households own at least one mobile phone, averages some 75 million SMS messages a month. U.S. carriers view SMS as a new revenue stream and they plan to promote its use over the next few years, targeting mainly business users and teenagers and young adults.

According to the 2001 Telecommunications Market Review and Forecast published by the U.S-based Telecommunications Industry Association (TIA), the success of free Internet in Europe is pushing interest in the free service model in the United States. "For wireless subscribers, having access to the Internet via wireless technology would not replace the traditional PC and fixed network model, but would satisfy consumers who are interested in SMS text messages," the TIA report states, adding that the rollout of SMS has accelerated the demand for e-mail access and information services in Europe.

Analysis, a U.K.-based market research organization, also believes that the success of SMS is tied to a great extent to the youth market. SMS, says Analysis, "is challenging the role of the passed note."

5.5 Are paging and short messaging good alternatives to cellular and PCS voice service?

Paging, probably the simplest method of delivering messages wirelessly today, is available with one- or two-way service and 100 percent coverage of the United States and most other countries. Paging services are available from a variety of carriers, including some FM broadcasters and mobile communications satellite services.

- Paging is the most reliable and cost-effective form of mobile communications today.

- Some cellular and PCS phones and PDAs have short messaging capability.

- Research In Motion Ltd. (RIM) is providing a secure version of its handheld BlackBerry unit for use by the U.S. government's Defense Message System.

- RIM and Lucent Technologies have formed an alliance to develop 3G messaging services.

Tell Me More

Paging continues to be the most reliable and cost-effective form of mobile communications in use today. At the low end, it is an inexpensive communications tool for consumers. At the high end, it is a convenient device for sending and receiving e-mail and other data. More than 50 million people subscribe to a one-way paging service worldwide, although advanced messaging systems are becoming a more popular alternative.

One-way pagers enable messages to be sent from a radio tower to a pager without a return acknowledgement signal. The market for one-way pagers has slipped in favor of two-way models, which permit users to respond to pages. Two-way voice pagers are also available that allow messages to be broadcast through a built-in speaker in the paging unit.

Paging and SMS differ in several ways. For one thing, paging operates on its own network. Also, different pagers use different technologies. Even if they share the same frequency, they might operate on a different communications protocol. This means that someone using a pager from one company might not be able to communicate with someone using a pager from another company.

SMS, which has its own interoperability issues in the United States because it operates over the European-developed Global System for Mobile Communications (GSM) digital cellular standard, gives users the ability to send and receive messages over GSM cellular and Personal Communications Service (PCS) networks. Also, people using pagers tend to leave them on all day, whereas many if not most cellphone users turn their phones on only when they are using them. However, SMS messages can still be received because the carriers provide a "store and forward" capability; in other words, messages can be stored while the phone is off and forwarded to the user when he or she checks for messages.

U.S. carriers and some cellphone manufacturers expect to get around the interoperability issue by developing and promoting products and services that use e-mail to send and receive messages over their cellphones and other wireless devices.

Some of the more recent pager/text messaging developments include:

- America Online's AOL Mobile Communicator is a two-way paging device developed by Research In Motion (RIM). This service allows subscribers to access only AOL instant messaging and e-mail services.

- For subscribers who require it, Research In Motion Ltd. (RIM) provides secure wireless access to the U.S. government's Defense Message System (DMS) via RIM's handheld BlackBerry wireless e-mail system. The system is designed to meet government standards for remote access to DMS, which is a global messaging system for the military and intelligence communities. DMS was initially designed for use by the allied countries and has been implemented by governments in the United States, Great Britain, and Canada. The new BlackBerry system provides several secure wireless features, including authentication of sender and receiver.

- RIM and Lucent Technologies have also formed an alliance to accelerate commercialization of next-generation mobile services using Lucent Technologies' wireless networks and RIM's products and services. The RIM and Lucent partnership spans three major wireless standards—cdma2000, General Packet Radio Service (GPRS), and Universal Mobile Telecommunications Systems (UMTS).

Chapter 6

Mobile Devices, Services, and Special Features

6.1 What are personal digital assistants?

Personal digital assistants (PDAs) originally served as electronic orga-nizers, or subnotebook computers. Today, they have much more func-tionality. They let you access, store, and organize information; many of them have clip-on cellphones, games, and other features, which puts them into a new class of products called "smart phones."

- Today's Palm-type PDAs offer several options and accessories, including GPS navigational modules, games, and Internet access.

- So-called smart phones, which integrate cellphones and PDAs into a single unit, have gained in popularity.

- There are several PDA model choices, but the trend is toward more highly integrated features.

Tell Me More

The Palm Pilot, Compaq's iPAQ, Kyocera's QCP, and most other PDAs available on the market today fit into a shirt pocket, and they can perform many of the functions of a desktop PC. They also can exchange data with desktop computers. With modules and other accessories, they offer such features as WAP services, address book and contacts, a calendar, a notepad, wireless Internet connections, and (in some attachable modules) MP3, and GPS navigational data.

So-called smart phones, which integrate cellphone and PDA functionality into a single unit, have gained the most interest. Market analysts are projecting that these dual functionality phone/PDAs will be the fastest-growing segment of the handheld device market, particularly among business or professional users who prefer to travel with a single device that can handle most of their portable communications and computing requirements. The newest smart phone models are lighter and easier-to-use than early versions, and they are less expensive.

The two most highly touted smart phones have been Kyocera's QCP 6035 and the Z100 Smartphone, developed by Sendo and based on the Microsoft smart phone platform, code-named "Stinger." The Sendo Z100 is a tri-band phone (that is, it can operate seamlessly in regions where wireless carriers offer service in the GSM 900, 1800, and 1900 MHz frequency bands) with a full color display, MP3, Windows Media audio files, and it comes with a stereo headset.

Another Palm-compatible PDA model by Handspring features e-mail and Web capabilities and a cellphone attachment. With the anticipated growth of mobile devices that combine phones and PDAs, virtually all cellphone manufacturers are designing products that integrate these functions.

Most PDAs feature PalmOS, the operating system, and Palm has long dominated this area. However, new products from Microsoft and Research In Motion (RIM) have softened Palm's market-leading position. Palm also expects to become a major vendor of handheld computers designed specifically for business applications, which can be managed by corporate information officers (CIOs). (According to Palm's customer surveys, more than 40 percent of Palm handhelds are paid for or reimbursed by companies, and 80 percent are synced at work.)

Using PDAs as a Learning Tool. Increasingly, PDAs, because of their growing technical capability, will be used as educational tools. Global-

LearningSystems (GLS), for example, offers an interactive training product for Palm, Compaq iPAQ, and HP Jornada PDA users. The system enables end users to download training programs into their PDA for offline viewing. Future applications will take advantage of wireless interconnectivity and Web-based interaction. In actual use, an insurance company, for example, could transmit program and policy changes and updates to its sales force. Similarly, changes in service or maintenance procedures could be sent directly to field service personnel.

Servers, which act as a central computer for storing and distributing data to many users at the same time, will play a larger role in this process. They have the ability to identify the type of PDA used and build and download Web pages that are particularly suited for the end user's device. This gives IT departments much needed flexibility with a workforce that may be equipped with many different types of mobile devices. Servers will also upload data from users' PDAs. Users of PDAs featuring PalmOS can receive content created with text, graphics, and simple interactivity. Users with Microsoft's Pocket PC OS have the added advantage of being able to receive full-motion video, animation, and sound clips.

eBooks on PDAs. The publishing world has been thinking about and promoting electronic books for at least a few years, but the installed base of e-books is still tiny. And it is still not clear how many people are willing to pay for a device that only allows them to read books on a small, sometimes hard to read, electronic display. Many marketers believe that PDAs, which in addition to having many other useful functions feature a larger display than most mobile products, may be the answer.

Palm has already licensed a wide variety of typical reference materials (dictionaries, encyclopedias, *Farmer's Almanac*, etc.) as eBook applications for their users. The eBooks can be read using optional media cards available for the Palm m500 series handheld computer. The cards are available from Franklin Electronic Publishers.

Franklin has begun to incorporate these MultiMediaCard memory cards into a few eBooks for its m500 series. The MultiMediaCard is a format for storing large amounts of data on mobile electronic products.

The format has the benefit of being compact and lightweight. Mobile devices based on the MultiMediaCard standard are being used in mobile devices, such as PDAs, portable computers, mobile phones, MP3 players, video game devices, and digital cameras.

The PalmPak Dictionary/Thesaurus Card will combine Merriam-Webster's Tenth Collegiate Dictionary with Franklin's American-English Thesaurus. The PalmPak Translator includes Franklin's English-French, English-Italian, English-German, and English-Spanish bi-directional translators.

Children's PDAs. There is also a category of PDAs designed specifically for children. Most of these are designed to look like handheld games. They include features such as instant messaging, built-in voice recorders, and video and audio functions to enable children to send digital pictures and notes with sound or to listen to MP3 files.

6.2 What are personalized mobile services?

Personalized mobile services enable wireless subscribers to customize the information they receive on their mobile handsets, including wireless phones, PDAs, and two-way messaging devices. These services can range from updates of scores of predesignated sports teams to such future location-based applications as alerting wireless device users that they are approaching a detour or construction site they may want to avoid.

- Several wireless carriers, Web portals, and information aggregators have developed personalized content services for their subscribers.

- Verizon mobile Web customers can access a variety of Web sites, ranging from personal finance and shopping to news and entertainment.

- Short Message Service (SMS) is also providing personalized data.

- Most personalized mobile services are offered on a local basis, but carriers are beginning to expand these services for their more mobile users.

■ Wireless carriers hope to introduce a much broader offering of personalized mobile services in the future.

Tell Me More

Several wireless carriers (including AT&T Wireless, Verizon Wireless, and Sprint PCS) have developed personalized Web portals to give their subscribers with Web-enabled wireless phones access to content on the Internet that is of interest to them, such as news, sports scores, weather reports, and movie listings. Yahoo, MSN, and Excite have also introduced services for Web-enabled phone users in the United States. Yahoo, for example, offers travel booking and travel information services as part of its Yahoo! Everywhere Wireless Initiative, a service designed specifically for wireless clients.

There are also information aggregators who provide personalized data for mobile users. One of these, Air2Web, offers a number of custom services, including wireless package tracking for United Parcel Services.

Through a series of agreements Verizon Wireless has made with Internet content providers, its Mobile Web customers can access a variety of Web sites, ranging from personal finance and shopping to news and entertainment. Users can customize the information they receive on the MyVZW.com Web site. Service options include updates on stock portfolios and having an alert sent when a particular stock reaches a target price point. Users can also comparison shop, book airline flights, make restaurant reservations, and receive a daily horoscope.

Short Message Service (SMS), which is available on a growing number of wireless devices, is also providing personalized data. For example, First Union and Citibank now offer e-mail and pager alerts via SMS to anyone using their PC banking services.

One of the downsides to personalized mobile services is that some of them are highly localized and do not always allow travelers to access their personalized information from anywhere. Another issue for many mobile users is the simple but tedious task of typing information requests using the tiny keyboards on mobile phones and other wireless devices. Future device designs may get around this issue; an obvious solution at some point would be to use speech recognition technology for inputting personal data requests.

With wireless carriers becoming increasingly aggressive about differentiating their services, wireless subscribers can expect to see more personalized location-based services in the future.

6.3 What is the status of voice or speech recognition?

Voice recognition is a technology that enables users to activate and/or control the functions of their cellular phones and other electronic devices by voice commands. Currently, mobile device users can check their e-mail, get information on stocks, sports, weather, driving directions and traffic conditions using voice recognition-enabled models. In the near future, voice portal companies will introduce more compelling and more highly featured voice-operated applications.

- Wireless is the major driver pushing new developments in voice recognition technologies.

- Market research indicates that the number of people using mobile voice portals—essentially gateways to the Web, a home site where surfers can go before looking for other sites—to access information on the Internet, will climb rapidly to 56 million in the United States by 2005.

- Legislation introduced on local and state levels to restrict the use of mobile phones while driving could further speed the development and acceptance of voice recognition technologies.

- Wireless carriers will promote voice-based services as a way of increasing their revenue.

- A relatively new organization, the VXML Forum, has been formed to develop and promote technical standards for voice recognition.

- One of the most popular mobile voice-recognition systems already in use is General Motors' OnStar, which is available on several top-of-the-line GM vehicles.

■ An emerging technology, known as "word spotting," has gained some attention for its ability to respond easily to key words and phrases.

Tell Me More

Mobile communications and the Internet are rapidly becoming major market drivers of new developments in speech recognition and other voice-related technologies. An important reason for this is that current user interfaces in mobile devices— mainly very small and hard to navigate keyboards—provide limited input and output.

The number of people using mobile voice portals to access information on the Internet is projected to grow from about one million in 2001 to more than 56 million by the end of 2005 in North America, with both enterprises and consumers playing key roles in the growth and development of voice portals.

Legislation restricting drivers' use of handheld phones was introduced in forty-three U.S. states in 2001, but only New York State has approved such a measure. Still, the interest in improving safety among cellphone users in vehicles is expected to speed the development of hands-free, voice-operated dialing.

Mobile device manufacturers are interested in voice-recognition because it meets the growing demand for hands-free operation, it potentially eliminates the need for extensive keying of buttons on small mobile devices, and it helps differentiate their products from their competitors.

Carriers will promote and deploy speech technologies to help users increase their productivity and to create new revenue streams from enhanced, mainly location-based, services by charging for voice-driven services, such as directions and traffic reports, or offering the service free to subscribers, but with pre-recorded advertisements paid for by restaurants and merchants. AT&T Wireless, Qwest Wireless, and Sprint PCS have launched voice-activated data services. AT&T's #121, Qwest's Voice Browsing, and Sprint PCS's Voice Command are considered safer and easier to use than pressing buttons because they allow users to simply speak into their cellular phones to call up voice recordings of news, weather, entertainment listings, and other information.

One of the most important developments in voice recognition is the formation of the VXML Forum to simplify the creation and delivery of Web-based, personalized interactive voice-response services developing VoiceXML (Voice eXtensible Markup Language), an open VXML specification for voice Web access. The forum was organized by Motorola, Lucent Technologies, AT&T, and IBM and now has nearly 400 company members. Wireless carriers such as Sprint and Verizon Wireless plan to offer services based on the VoiceXML standard by the end of 2001.

A variety of voice applications are in use and planned with a great deal of attention focused on making the Internet more easily accessible by mobile phone. One speech recognition feature that is gaining in popularity is part of General Motors' hands-free, in-vehicle OnStar information system. Other systems will enable mobile customers to access more than 300 different databases, including restaurant guides, yellow and white pages, and other information by subscriber preference.

Another technology that is available to mobile communications device manufacturers is known as "word spotting." Word spotting enables common electronic devices—such as mobile phones, answering machines and other devices—to respond to a user's utterance of a key word or phrase, even when embedded within the middle of a sentence. For example, a telephone could be trained to respond to the phrase "make a call." When using the phrase, "I'd like to make a call now," word spotting technology would pick up the gateway phrase "make a call" within the sentence and then prompt the user for a name or number to dial.

Word spotting is an early example of voice recognition technologies that will allow users to "speech surf"—speak commands rather than keying them into mobile communications/computing information devices.

6.4 When will video services be widely available?

Mobile video is available with a few portable/mobile devices, but it is not quite ready for prime time. Video requires more bandwidth, or throughput, to transmit video information (usually expressed in kilobits or megabits per second) and wireless services have not been assigned enough bandwidth at this point to make mobile video an important feature for business users or consumers.

- Mobile video pictures are jerky, and the very small screens on most mobile and portable devices are not very popular with people used to viewing video on large screens.

- A single technical standard to ensure that video is interoperable across all mobile devices is recognized as a key requirement.

- The most popular applications are expected to be business and entertainment related, including news, sports features, and games.

- The current and widely accepted standard for mobile video is MPEG-4, which has won the approval of the International Telecommunications Union (ITU).

- PacketVideo is working with several equipment manufacturers and wireless carriers to bring full-motion video to mobile devices.

- Sprint PCS has already begun field testing of streaming video for its mobile subscribers.

- At least two industry organizations have been formed to promote mobile video and technical standards.

Tell Me More

Getting mobile video to where it needs to be technically for wide acceptance will be a challenge. Currently, the best these systems can offer is short video clips and still images, and these are not good quality transmissions by accepted consumer standards. The technology is in what most key players would refer to as the "advanced prototype" phase. All of the basic technical elements or enabling technologies exist for real-time mobile streaming video (real-time streaming means that the video can be viewed as it is being transmitted rather than waiting for a complete "file" to be downloaded). However, the wireless infrastructure—mainly transmission speeds, connection speeds while roaming, distance from the antenna, and image quality—continues to require development. Also, packaging these technologies into small, lightweight mobile or portable products represents a design challenge.

Success for vendors in this field requires that they agree to ensure that their products meet a single technical standard—in other words, that they are interoperable. It will also require that they develop useful applications for the business/professional community as well as the mass consumer market.

Application possibilities run the gamut from receiving business-related and entertainment features and games to news and sports features. The technology will, in time, enable mobile users to receive pay-per-view programming and personalized video messages and participate in video conferences while on the road. It may also be possible to view traffic on specific roads and streets from miles away by pressing a single pre-programmed key, or by simply speaking the name of the road into the mobile device.

Currently, the designated standard for mobile video applications is MPEG-4 (Motion Picture Experts Group-4). It has already been defined and accepted by the International Telecommunications Union (ITU), the telecom standards-setting arm of the United Nations. A great deal of research and development work is already underway to make mobile video a reality under MPEG-4 specifications.

PacketVideo, which develops MPEG-4-compliant software for delivering video and audio over mobile networks, is working with several equipment manufacturers and wireless carriers to bring full-motion video to mobile devices, including Internet-enabled wireless phones, PDAs, and laptops. Qualcomm is integrating streaming video capabilities into its chips and system software for CDMA phones. Agere Systems (formerly Lucent Technologies' Microelectronics Group) has similar plans for next-generation mobile phones. Toshiba and Siemens have formed a global alliance to integrate streaming video technologies into their future phones. Motorola plans to plug video into its iDEN phones. Palm has announced plans to offer video on its PDAs. Sony has demonstrated a version of the Palm PDA with a video playback capability for clips and still pictures.

Media and online companies are also planning to develop content for new mobile video services. At least one U.S. carrier, Sprint PCS, has begun testing wireless streaming video for multimedia applications and audio services for current wireless devices. Japan's Personal Handy-phone Service (PHS) carriers are already streaming short promotional videos, such as movie trailers and other short subjects, and expect to add longer video features in the future, for which they may charge at least a small fee.

At least two industry organizations have sprung up to help promote mobile video technologies and to develop compatible video standards. One is the Wireless Multimedia Forum, or WMF (www.wmmforum.com), the other is the Internet Streaming Media Alliance (www.ism-alliance.org). The WMF has already produced Version 1.0 of its Recommended Technical Framework Document, which defines the file format between non-mobile multimedia distribution servers that store and distribute key audio and video files and wireless multimedia terminals, such as cellular phones and PDAs.

6.5 Why is improving display technologies important?

One of the issues that is always raised in any discussion of why mobile data and Internet-enabled devices aren't growing as fast as some market analysts have projected is the display. Cellular phone and PDA displays are simply too small to project the growing amount and variety of text and graphics information that mobile users can now access.

User expectations of high quality images, forged by years of looking at bright, large computer screens, fairly high resolution TV sets, and personal computer monitors, are high. As a result, the availability and growth of e-mail and Internet browsing mobile phones is putting pressure on manufacturers to produce easier to read microdisplays.

- The visual interface is becoming increasingly important to the development of new and emerging mobile Internet devices.

- Virtual displays can make display screens appear larger than they are.

- Display modules that are a half-inch diagonal in size offer a resolution of 480,000 pixels.

■ One of the more unique new display devices looks like oversized sunglasses. They are actually highly miniaturized versions of the "head-up" displays that fighter aircraft pilots use to view critical information on the cockpit canopies. These displays reduce the need for pilots to look down at their instrument panel during combat maneuvers.

■ Another new device is a handheld unit with a touchpad and monocle-like eyepiece for viewing personal data.

■ More color displays are becoming available on mobile devices, but they are also more costly and tend to drain batteries very rapidly.

■ Mobile video is available on a few devices, but its quality still leaves a lot to be desired.

Tell Me More

From an industrial design point of view, the visual interface is becoming increasingly important to the design and development of new and emerging mobile Internet appliances. Product designers now have far more options, including the use of color displays and a choice of display technologies that offer varying degrees of brightness, ruggedness, battery life, and cost.

One of the emerging developments in microdisplays is the so-called virtual display, which features near-to-eye optical magnifiers similar to those used in video camcorders that make text, maps, and data-packed business graphics easier to read in portable electronic products. Optically-aided viewfinders make the display screen appear larger than it actually is.

Currently, some fifteen companies are developing these new miniature displays, which have begun to appear in some specialized products, including mobile phones, digital still cameras, and camcorders. Using a cellular phone with a virtual display, for example, an architect standing at a construction site could discuss changes in a blueprint with a colleague who is back at the office. The architect in the field could view the entire blueprint through the virtual display.

Display modules are now available that are one-half inch diagonally in size with a resolution of 480,000 pixels. When used with optical enhancements, the display is a virtual image equivalent to viewing an entire 19-inch diagonal monitor.

One of the more unique display products looks like a slightly over-sized pair of sunglasses, but is actually a smaller version of a "head-up" computer display. Available from Inviso, these eShades are being marketed for use with mobile phones, PDAs, digital cameras, and handheld Internet appliances. Another new device is eCase, a handheld unit with a touchpad and a helmet- or hat-mounted flip up/down monocle-like eyepiece for viewing personal files and other data.

Both of these devices are expected to be popular with anyone who wants privacy while viewing computer data—for example, working on a laptop computer or PDA while sitting on an airplane.

Color displays are an important development because they are often easier to read and offer new ways to present information, particularly for charts, graphs, and tables. There are downsides with color displays in mobile devices, however, and they include the added manufacturing cost (which increases the sales price) and the fact that batteries drain noticeably faster than with monochrome displays.

Still, most of the leading mobile phone and PDA vendors plan to offer MPEG-4-supported streaming video in their future products.

A few new mobile applications, such as the UP Browser micro-browser for Wireless Application Protocol (WAP)-enabled devices, allow users to select their color display preferences. Also, Handspring has introduced Visor Prism, a color-screen PDA with a built-in lithium-ion rechargeable battery to compensate at least partially for the additional power drain. Kyocera also markets a mobile phone with a built-in video viewer.

Handheld video displays present another opportunity for mobile device manufacturers to differentiate their products and for giving users new options. Some products are available with short, but choppy looking videoclips. Full-motion video is still in development and subject to many variables, including the ability of the network carrier to provide bandwidth and data speeds to accommodate appropriate frame rates for useful video viewing.

6.6 What is Bluetooth?

Bluetooth is a short-range (about ten meters) digital transmission standard aimed at providing a wireless link between laptop computers, cellular phones, and other wireless devices. In what Bluetooth developers call "unconscious" or "hidden" computing, Bluetooth-enabled products can automatically seek each other out and configure themselves into networks.

Originally conceived as a replacement for short cable connections, the key characteristic of Bluetooth-enabled devices is that they can detect and communicate with other similarly-enabled devices within a limited range—all without conscious user intervention. In other words, Bluetooth devices can detect other Bluetooth devices and start "talking" to each other once within range. However, to avoid exchanging information (such as personal or business data) with everyone you might pass in a hallway or on the street, you have to give permission for the device to identify you to anyone or another Bluetooth device.

- Bluetooth is a radio and therefore works over longer ranges than other technologies. It does not need to be pointed in the direction of another device to send or receive information.

- Interference may be a problem.

- Security, including the use of encrypted data, has been designed into the Bluetooth technical specification.

- Industry analysts are projecting that more than one billion Bluetooth-enabled devices will be in use by the end of 2005.

Tell Me More

Unlike infrared (IR) technologies, which are purely directional (your TV remote, for example, is an IR device) and operate over a very short range, Bluetooth can operate at up to 10 meters (eventually up to 100 meters in future versions). Since it is a radio, it does not need to be pointed directly at another Bluetooth-enabled device to communicate.

A number of technical issues have been advanced for Bluetooth, but are expected to be resolved before Bluetooth devices reach the market in any significant numbers. One of these issues is interference. Bluetooth operates at 2.4 GHz, the same radio frequency as microwave ovens, wireless local area networks, wireless home networks, and some cordless phones, garage door openers, and toys. However, because of its short range and the design of its system architecture, Bluetooth advocates don't expect interference to be a problem in actual use.

Engineers at Lucent Technologies have also disclosed potential leaks in Bluetooth security, an obvious concern among users who may want to exchange company or personal data in a public place. However, the Bluetooth Special Interest Group (SIG) has indicated that future versions of Bluetooth (e.g., those that will soon reach the mass market) will be protected from hacking.

Critical mass is key for Bluetooth to succeed. Market projections for Bluetooth have been huge, ranging up to more than a billion Bluetooth-enabled mobile devices sold by the end of 2005. With more than 2,000 member companies participating in the Bluetooth SIG, all aggressively designing Bluetooth products and promoting the technology, and with new generations of wireless products hitting the market just about every six months or so, this projection may not be far off.

6.7 What will Bluetooth be used for?

Bluetooth technology will soon appear in mobile phones and handheld computers, digital cameras, security systems, and office equipment, among many other devices. But even Bluetooth's strongest advocates have only begun to consider the possibilities for Bluetooth technology. With Bluetooth, you can send e-mail from the computer on your lap to your cellular phone or PDA in your briefcase. That information can be automatically synchronized with your desktop PC whenever you pass it within Bluetooth range. You can order candy or a soft drink from a Bluetooth-equipped vending machine by using a Bluetooth-enabled mobile device. Bluetooth will also work in a fixed environment; for example, to send data via wall-mounted access points in airports, hotels, and conference centers.

■ Bluetooth-linked cellphones or PDAs can automatically synchronize with desktop PCs.

■ Bluetooth technology can be embedded into a wide variety of
portable and fixed wireless applications and devices.

■ In the not-too-distant future, Bluetooth will enable wireless "road
warriors" to check their e-mail at airports, conference centers,
and in hotels via special wall-mounted access points, eliminating
the need to plug their laptops and other mobile devices into a
data port.

Tell Me More

Several Bluetooth products have already been introduced, including a
headset, a PC Card for laptops and PDAs, and cellphones. A Bluetooth
keyboard and mouse have been announced as future products. In addition, Nokia and Fujifilm are working on a mobile imaging technology
that would enable Nokia to add a Bluetooth chip to its clamshell-shaped
9110 Communicator so that it could receive images taken on a Bluetooth-equipped Fujifilm digital camera.

A Bluetooth-linked cellphone or PDA can automatically synchronize with a desktop personal computer when they pass within Bluetooth range. The Holiday Inn Wall Street, which bills itself as "the most
technologically sophisticated hotel in New York," already allows you to
check into your room simply by walking past the front desk with a Bluetooth-enabled and activated device. Your pre-registration information is
transmitted immediately and automatically. All you need is a room key.

The device could be a cellphone, a Palm-type handheld personal
computer, or a laptop or notebook computer. The Holiday Inn is using
Registry Magic's Consumer Payment Network to implement the Bluetooth network. Essentially, your Bluetooth device replaces your wallet,
using a personal code to identify you to the hotel the moment you're in
range of the hotel desk. Similarly, you can order a soft drink or candy
from a Bluetooth-enabled vending machine by simply signaling an
account code from a Bluetooth cellphone or PDA. Your account would
be debited based on your code. Eventually, Bluetooth-equipped cell

phones and PDAs will be able to display personal bar codes, which can be read by a vending machine scanner.

Other Bluetooth-enabled devices will include headsets for hands-free cellphone use and for video and audio systems, toys and games, medical devices, and even non-mobile or portable devices, such as security systems, digital cameras, and office products (printers, scanners, fax machines).

Bluetooth also lends itself to a combination of mobile or portable and fixed wireless applications. For instance, in the not-too-distant future, access points (essentially special Bluetooth antennas that look like smoke alarms) will be installed at airports, hotels, and conference centers. This will enable anyone with a mobile Bluetooth-enabled device, such as a cellphone, two-way messaging device, or laptop computer, to send and receive data without having to search for and connect their device to a data port.

6.8 How does Bluetooth help create more broadly defined wireless personal area networks?

One development with a potentially significant impact on Bluetooth and other personal area networks is the work of the Institute of Electrical and Electronic Engineers' (IEEE) 802.15 Wireless Personal Area Network (WPAN) Task Group. Formed in late 1999, the group was borne out of an industry concern that various wireless devices and services based on several standards or specifications can peacefully coexist within the same 2.4 GHz frequency band.

- The IEEE 802.15 task group initially set out to develop a 1 mbps standard based on the work of the Bluetooth Special Interest Group (SIG).

- The group hopes to provide the foundation for developing a common technical interoperable standard for wireless personal area networks.

- Based on industry support and increasing interest in unlicensed wireless applications, the 802.15 group has formed two additional working groups, a coexistence task group and a high-rate study group.

Tell Me More

IEEE 802.15 began by developing a 1 mbps standard based on the work of the Bluetooth SIG. From there, it went on to develop a project definition for a consumer-priced, 20 mbps or faster, high-rate WPAN that can be widely deployed for short-range information transfer, particularly multimedia and digital imaging.

The task group's definition of a WPAN is a low-cost networking scheme that enables computing devices such as PCs, laptop computers, printers, and PDAs to wirelessly communicate with each other over short distances.

The IEEE's goal is to provide the foundation for a broad range of interoperable consumer devices by establishing universally-adopted standards and recommended practices for wireless digital communications. The creation of a WPAN protocol is a critical part of this approach. The anticipated draft standard, 802.15.1, will be a fully interoperable derivative of the Bluetooth specification.

Based on strong industry support and interest in increasing both the robustness of wireless solutions and data rates, two additional groups working on standards have been formed.

Coexistence Task Group. A major concern that had been shared by many in the industry is whether various wireless devices based on several standards or specifications can coexist within the same 2.4 GHz frequency band. The 802.15 Coexistence Task Group (TG2) will address the issue of coexistence between WPANs and other wireless devices, such as IEEE 802.11 wireless local area networks, Bluetooth, HomeRF, some of the newer cordless phones, and some garage door openers and toys. Microwave ovens operate at 2.4 GHz as well. IEEE 802.11 is a wireless version of the Ethernet local area networks deployed in offices and other business facilities. Updated versions of Bluetooth, including new security features, have addressed this issue and presumably will significantly reduce, if not eliminate, this potential problem.

Initially, the TG2 will attempt first to understand the effects of mutual interference and then subsequently to produce a recommended practice for WPAN devices operating in the wireless local area network environment. An extended vision of the TG2 is to assist standards development in minimizing the potential for interference among different radio systems in the unlicensed bands.

802.15 High Rate Study Group. This group is addressing the technical merits and market requirements for a low cost, high data rate WPAN. It has developed a Project Authorization Request (PAR) so that a new task group within 802.15 can begin work on a draft standard.

Initial meetings of the 802.15 Working Group outlined a data rate of 1 Mbps for WPANs. The new High Speed Study Group, however, will seek to provide high-speed physical (PHY) and medium access control (MAC) layers to support multimedia data types and data rates of 20 Mbps or more. Compatibility with other 802.15 standards is a major goal of this activity.

The high-speed group says its work is necessary because current standards and data rates do not meet the projected needs of multimedia and digital imaging in consumer-class products, such as digital cameras. Speed, battery life, and ultra low cost are the key requirements in this product category rather than range.

6.9 What is the future of mobile gaming and entertainment?

The popularity of mobile gaming and entertainment is expected to be a driving force in the development of mobile technology, particularly in handheld devices with strong communications and computing capability.

- An industry initiative is underway to define a universal mobile games platform.

- Nokia is using the Global System for Mobile Communications to deploy its mobile entertainment service throughout Europe.

- Motorola is working with Sega Enterprises and Digital Bridges to create entertainment software for Java-based mobile devices.

- A number of technical barriers to growth must still be addressed if mobile gaming and other forms of entertainment are to be successful and grow.

- Building a revenue base is one of the biggest challenges facing online game companies.

Tell Me More

Industry analyst Datamonitor valued the global mobile gaming market in 1999 at $2.9 billion. By 2005, it expects four out of five mobile phone users will be playing wireless games. From a more anecdotal perspective, analysts highlight the market potential of mobile gaming by noting that sales of computer games in 2000 nearly matched movie box-office receipts. This experience, they believe, will spill over to mobile devices.

In Japan, an estimated 55 percent of the content that subscribers access through NTT DoCoMo's wireless Internet i-mode is entertainment. The i-mode service is scheduled to become available in the United States by late 2001 or early 2002 through a multi-billion dollar investment by NTT DoCoMo in AT&T Wireless.

Wireless network operators and software developers are faced with an overwhelming array of choices for mobile game services. At present there is no open, nonproprietary standard and extensible platform for mobile gaming. Without such a platform, network operators face greater complexity and cost in offering a wide range of games that access their systems, such as billing, authentication, and location services. Without a standard, developers of mobile games are faced with writing their own platforms or having to multiply the efforts to support many platforms. Wireless networking operators and software developers are faced with an overwhelming array of choices for mobile gaming services, but the focus seems to be on real-time games accessed from Short Messaging Services (SMS) or from the Internet. Downloadable (over-the-air) games are also expected to increase in popularity.

Against that background, Ericsson, Motorola, and Siemens Information and Communication Mobile are working together to define a universal mobile games platform. To help speed up the process and maintain some commonality, they are drawing from existing and emerging technical standards. Eventually, Ericsson, Motorola, and Siemens hope to work with other industry leaders to enhance and promote their new universal game platform.

By creating a standardized platform for mobile gaming applications, mobile network operators and application service providers (ASPs) believe that consumers worldwide will have access to a wide variety of engaging interactive mobile games.

WAP-enabled games. Nokia's new Mobile Entertainment Service has been deployed on Global System for Mobile Communications (GSM) digital cellular networks throughout Europe. The service allows game application developers and online content publishers to create interactive games and other entertainment features for Wireless Application Protocol (WAP)-enabled devices. More than 300 companies have registered for the program. One company, Activision, plans to convert its popular *Hitchhiker's Guide to the Galaxy* into a WAP-enabled game.

Java-based games. Motorola has joined with Sega Enterprises to create entertainment software for Java technology-enabled mobile phones, pagers, and PDAs. Motorola is also working with UK-based Digital Bridges, a specialist in wireless games, to develop single- and multi-player Java-based games.

On the carrier side, Verizon Wireless has signed on Boxerjam, a developer of games, to provide Verizon's mobile Web customers with two new games. The games can be accessed through the entertainment section of the Websites on Internet-ready mobile handsets.

There are some technical issues that need to be addressed before mobile gaming can meet current market projections for its growth. For one thing, broadband services will have to be available to accommodate the download speeds necessary to satisfy mobile gamers. Game files can be huge. Whereas most of the games that are currently available are relatively simple, the newer games will grow in complexity. Consumers will demand more challenging and interesting games. Interactive mobile gaming devices will need to take advantage of improving local storage and memory capacity technologies to handle these more complex games.

Revenue-generating business models for network operators are expected to vary as mobile games and other interactive entertainment features become more readily available and as the market matures. In fact, studies by International Data Corp. (IDC) indicate that building a revenue base is one of the biggest challenges facing online gaming companies, mainly because wireless subscribers, particularly those in the United States, are used to receiving so many services free. According to one recent IDC study, "Because advertising revenue, which most business models are currently built on, could dry up in the future, many sites are looking to create more attractive advertisement opportunities beyond banner ads through sponsorship and targeted ads and are trying to migrate free subscribers to paid subscribers." Other activities, such as licensing technology and co-branding games, could also open up revenue opportunities.

IDC also believes that companies will expand their business models by developing unique and appealing nontraditional games that are designed specifically for use with mobile phones and PDAs.

6.10 What are the prospects for mobile access to music?

Despite the well-publicized legal difficulties of Napster and MP3.com, Inc., the technology to allow users to facilitate the delivery and storage of virtually any type of audio service, including music, remains a viable opportunity for a growing number innovative mobile network carriers and online services.

- MP3.com, Inc. is working with Qualcomm to develop music applications for wireless devices.

- A federal court ruling on Napster may force content providers to ensure security of any material distributed over the Internet.

Tell Me More

Technology will enable consumers to travel with their favorite music. Users may be able to access their personal music collection in their My.MP3 account on their wireless device. MP3.com's vision also aims to provide audio greeting cards and the ability to browse for music genres via wireless devices.

MP3 stands for Motion Picture Expert Group (MPEG) 1, Layer 3. MPEG developed the MP3 technical standard to store music files on computer disks in a digital format. Since this takes up a lot of space, the digital data is compressed for storage. MP3 is very popular because the music stored in MP3 files offers very high quality sound. MP3 is available as a feature application on a growing number of new mobile devices, including cellphones, PDAs, and of course, dedicated MP3 players. However, while it is legal to encode MP3 files from your own CDs for your own use, it is illegal to trade them with others unless you have copyright permission to do so.

The MP3.com company has demonstrated a prototype of what it calls MP3 Mobile, using its Music InterOperating System to deliver music from mobile devices via Qualcomm, Inc.'s Binary Runtime Environment for Wireless (BREW). This works with the Qualcomm-developed code division multiple access (CDMA) digital transmission system for cellular phones. BREW enables users to download applications wirelessly. It also provides a standard programming environment, which, according to Qualcomm, enables software developers to develop applications for all BREW-enabled phones rather than tweaking their software to make it work with any cellular phone or other wireless device.

MP3.com is offering manufacturers and network operators advanced tools and applications for integrating personalized audio content into their wireless handsets, car stereo systems, and other mobile devices. Verizon Wireless, Leap Communications, Samsung, Kyocera Wireless, and Korea Telecom have already signed up to develop services using the MP3.com/Qualcomm process.

MP3.com believes that it has the largest collection of digital music available on the Internet, with more than 967,000 songs and audio files posted from more than 150,000 digital artists and record labels.

The federal court ruling that Napster is responsible for protecting the copyright of music shared by its members is expected to put new pressure on online content vendors to protect the audio content distributed over the Internet. The ruling, in February 2001, affirms that vendors and distributors are legally and financially liable for the unauthorized (or, what is considered to be the unethical) downloading or sharing of online content. With the Napster ruling, the court is not seeking to stop peer-to-peer sharing of content (what academics and others have been doing for years), but it does protect artists, authors, and other content developers from uncontrolled and illegal distribution.

MP3.com's new operating system, Music InterOperating System (IOS) Application Programming Interface (API), is available for free download. The site is developer.mp3.com. This OS will allow next-generation handheld devices (including wireless), Internet appliances, software applications, and Web sites to handle the ever-growing number of MP3.com audio files. Through the service, customers can store and manage their music collections online through a password-protected account. For equipment manufacturers, the advantage of integrating the Music IOS API into their products will be that consumers with these new products will have access to hundreds of thousands of tracks from MP3.com's database of music.

MP3 is supported mostly by advertising revenue. Also, MP3.com stores files of top tunes on its own computers, allowing access only to songs that consumers already own, and it charges for this service. MP3.com's revenues for fiscal year 2000 were $80 million, although it reported a loss for that year.

Chapter 7

Cellular Communications and Specialized Mobile Radio

7.1 What is the history of cellular communications?

Cellular communications service started in the United States in Chicago in October 1983, shortly after the service was launched in Japan. The sequence of events leading to the development and actual deployment of cellular radio required several years.

- Much of the research for cellular radio evolved out of work done for military programs.

- AT&T was responsible for the first mobile telephone system connected to the public telephone network.

- It took twenty-five years to develop the technique of "handing off" mobile calls from one cell to another cell.

- In 1973, Motorola demonstrated a mobile phone that worked on the AT&T mobile telephone system.

- In 1981, the Federal Communications Commission (FCC) approved two cellular radio licenses in each market region in the United States

- By 1990, a license had been issued for at least one system in each U.S. market.

Tell Me More

Cellular service developed as an offspring of earlier work (much of it done by the U.S. military during and shortly after World War II) and of research undertaken by some of the biggest names in the radio industry, mainly AT&T and Motorola.

AT&T recognized the commercial potential for mobile communications in the early 1940s. By 1946, the company had created what it called Improved Mobile Telephone Service. IMTS was the first mobile radio system connected to the public telephone network. AT&T quickly won approval from the FCC to operate the first commercial public radio service in St. Louis. The service soon spread to twenty-five cities using high-power transmitters with a radius of about fifty miles each.

Incredibly, it took another twenty-five years to develop the technology that would enable mobile radio subscribers to "hand off" calls from one cell—a geographic area of multiple and overlapping cells that is served by a single low-powered transmitter/receiver—to another cell. Calls are switched from one transmitter to another as the mobile phone passes from one cell to another.

By 1973, Motorola had demonstrated a mobile phone that worked with the AT&T-developed network. In 1977, the FCC authorized two experimental licenses, one for Chicago, the other for the Baltimore/Washington, D.C. area. Then, in 1981, the Commission approved two licenses in each market area—one to a wireline company (meaning a telephone carrier that uses cables, not radio) and the other to a non-wireline, or cellular service, provider. In reality, both of these systems may be owned by the same company.

Finally, the FCC announced that it would award cellular radio licenses through a lottery system. By 1990, licenses had been issued for at least one system in every market in the United States today, cellular is available virtually worldwide.

7.2 What are the primary cellular technical standards and how do they work?

There are actually several technical analog and digital standards in the world. They use different radio frequency (RF) modulation techniques and operate at different frequencies.

- There are now four major technical cellular phone standards in the United States.

- The U.S. cellular standards are usually referred to in short-hand terms. They are AMPs, TDMA, CDMA and GSM.

Tell Me More

There are four basic standard systems currently in use in the United States. They are the original cellular system, known as Advanced Mobile Phone Service (AMPS), which began operations in the United States in October 1983, and three much more recently developed, but incompatible digital systems: time division multiple access (TDMA), code division multiple access (CDMA), and the Global System for Mobile Communications (GSM).

Advanced Mobile Phone Service. AMPS is the technical standard for analog cellular phones. It is the original cellular system in North America, Latin America, Australia, and parts of Russia and Asia. AMPS is available on virtually every cellular phone sold in the United States today, including every digital model. If digital service is not available in a particular region of the country, the phone will automatically switch to AMPS.

Time Division Multiple Access. TDMA is a digital technology that increases the channel capacity of TDMA-based cellular phones by splitting the frequency band into a number of channels; these in turn are stacked into short time slots so that several calls can share a single channel without interfering with each other. Current technology divides the channel into three time slots, each lasting a fraction of a second. Thus, a single channel can be used to handle three simultaneous calls. The Universal Wireless Communications Consortium, which promotes TDMA technology, says subscribers on its networks increased 74 percent to 61 million in 2000.

Code Division Multiple Access. CDMA is a digital technology that uses a low-power signal that is spread across a wide bandwidth. With CDMA, a phone call is assigned a code rather than to a certain frequency. Using the identifying code and a low-power signal, ten or more callers can use the same group of channels. Its unique code system "spreads" the signal across a wide area of the spectrum (a technique known as "spread spectrum"). A version of this so-called frequency-hopping technique was used for the first time during World War II to eliminate the jamming of radio control signals to torpedoes and to maintain secure radio communications. The CDMA Development Group says the number of wireless customers on its networks worldwide through October of 2000 was 71 million, up 73 percent from October 1999. The group also reported that 22 million subscribers are using wireless Internet services on CDMA networks.

Global System for Mobile Communications. GSM is a TDMA-based digital technology that is the pan-European technical standard for digital mobile telephony. It is also used in several other regions of the world, including some areas of the United States. However, GSM operates at different frequencies in the United States and Europe, Asia, and Australia. In this system, users share a frequency band and each user's speech is stored, compressed, and transmitted as a quick packet of information. The packet is decompressed at the receiving end of the transmission.

Originally called Groupe Speciale Mobile, GSM, like other digital systems, has more capacity than analog systems—up to eight users can share a single channel. As of January 2001, there were more than 456 million GSM customers in the world, mostly in Europe, but also in Africa, Asia, and the Middle East. According to the GSM Association, its system accounts for approximately 70 percent of the total digital cellular wireless market.

7.3 What is the difference between cellular phones and Personal Communications Service?

Cellular phones operate in small, geographic "cells," each of which is equipped with a low-power radio transmitter/receiver, which can be analog or digital. The cell can vary by size depending on terrain, capacity demands, and other technical issues. As mobile phones move from one cell to another, a computer at a Mobile Telephone Switching Office (MTSO) monitors their movement and, at an appropriate time, transfers, or "hands off," the phone call to the new cell, allowing the call to continue.

Personal Communications Service (PCS) is an inherently digital system. PCS cells, the geographic areas that are served by a single transmitter/receiver, are smaller than cellular cells, which means that more PCS cell sites are needed to cover the same area that is covered by cellular sites. However, PCS operates at a higher frequency than cellular (1.8 to 2 GHz for PCS compared to 800 MHz for cellular), so that PCS requires less power to operate.

- The FCC authorized PCS in the mid-1990s to create a more competitive mobile communications marketplace.

- PCS originated from a study published by the U.K. Department of Trade and Industry.

- The British government approved the deployment of so-called telepoint service, essentially a short-range, portable cordless phone that could originate, but not receive, calls.

- The rest of the world's telecom community took notice of the U.K.'s new service and, in the United States, the FCC authorized experimental field trials of what became a national deployment of PCS.

Tell Me More

The FCC authorized PCS in 1994 primarily to enhance the capacity of the wireless radio spectrum, and to boost competition for wireless services. The FCC allocated the 1910–1930 MHz frequency band for unlicensed PCS, which consists of wireless voice, data, and messaging services.

PCS extends the capacity of the system because a channel can transmit multiple signals simultaneously. Prior to the introduction of PCS, there were up to two cellular carriers in each market region; however, the Federal Communications Commission (FCC) has authorized up to six PCS carriers in each market.

When it was introduced, wireless carriers viewed PCS as an opportunity to expand and protect their markets with a new all-digital service at even lower subscriber rates than cellular. However, PCS has been difficult to differentiate from cellular service because industry analysts and the media have often referred to it as "cellular at a different frequency." In fact, functionally, cellular and PCS are very similar and many cellular carriers now offer PCS.

There are two types of PCS. Unlicensed PCS consists of wireless voice, data, and messaging systems and devices and is used for on-site or campus-wide service. A second type, broadband licensed PCS, provides wide-area services.

PCS grew out of a U.K. Department of Trade and Industry report published in 1989 called "Phones on the Move: Personal Communications in the 1990s." Just seven pages long, the report essentially jump-started the telecom community in the United Kingdom into providing mobile communications for the masses. The report stated: "More and more U.K. business is coming to rely on mobile communications, and government has acted as an enabler, making sure they get the services they need...."

The British government responded to the study by quickly licensing four companies to provide what were called telepoint or CT-2 (for cordless telephone, second generation) mobile communication services. Using what amounted to a wireless pay phone, subscribers could originate, but not receive, short-range phone calls in public areas equipped with telepoint base stations, such as train stations, airports, and busy shopping centers. Telepoint made sense in London, which had few pay phones. Unfortunately, the high subscriber cost ($200 for a handset, plus a sixty dollar service connection fee and a monthly service charge of fifteen dollars) did not sell well in a weak British economy. Despite these problems, the introduction of telepoint in the U.K. provided a wake-up call for the telecommunications world for the need for much broader wireless services.

In the United States, the FCC responded by issuing more than 200 experimental licenses for testing PCS in markets throughout the country. Cellular telephone carriers, cable television system operators, independent telecom system service providers, and telecom equipment manufacturers spent millions of dollars to develop and deploy new PCS products and services. In 2001, the U.S.-based Telecommunications Industry Association projected that industry spending on PCS would nearly triple to $46.4 billion by 2004.

7.4 What is Specialized Mobile Radio?

Specialized Mobile Radio (SMR) was created in 1974 by the Federal Communications Commission (FCC) to provide commercial dispatch services for business users, such as delivery trucks and taxies. Initially a voice network, the system has been upgraded in recent years to handle data between mobile workers and a central computer or dispatch station.

- Some very large companies have developed their own SMR systems.

- Most SMR services are offered in a limited geographic area.

- Nextel is the dominant SMR player in the United States.

Tell Me More

Most SMR providers are very small and offer service in a limited area. The one exception to this is Nextel Communications, which is the dominant player in the market. Nextel offers an "enhanced SMR service" called the Nextel Wireless Web. It provides customers with customer relationship management (CRM)-type solutions that enable mobile sales representatives, field technicians, and dispatchers in the cable and satellite television business to more quickly respond to customer service calls. Some companies have developed their own SMR systems. One example is Federal Express, which uses the wireless technology to keep track of its vehicles and packages.

FedEx has its own remote parcel-tracking system. In addition, rather than send its trucks out on a regular basis to check on the contents of its widely disbursed drop-boxes (some of which may be empty and therefore not worth the trip), FedEx has equipped some of these boxes with small, solar-powered radio transmitters to signal a dispatch center when a package has actually been dropped into the box.

United Parcel Service (UPS) has operated a nationwide, real-time package-tracking system for nearly ten years. It combines the company's existing wireline-based network with cellular technology. UPS says it now plans to introduce the world's largest consolidated wireless network, using Bluetooth radio technology. UPS package sorters will wear a ring to scan parcel barcodes. The ring will send a radio signal to a wireless terminal worn on the sorter's belt, eliminating straps and cords. The system will be tied into the UPS wireless local area network. The new system is expected to cost more than $100 million, an investment UPS expects to recover in less than a year through productivity gains.

Nextel uses Motorola's integrated digital enhanced network (iDEN) technology, which provides digital mobile phones with messaging capabilities. It also has a direct connect two-way radio feature that enables an individual to communicate with up to one hundred coworkers simultaneously.

In addition to handling update tasks, contacts, and sales leads in the CRM system, the Nextel eDispatch system provides installers and technicians with direct access to job and customer information and their company's customer management and billing system.

7.5 Why is digital technology important?

On a very practical level, there are several advantages in digital mobile service that set it apart from analog technologies. These include enhanced radio frequency spectrum capacity, higher speed data transmission, improved sound quality, longer battery life, and a higher level of privacy and security.

- Digital wireless technologies offer new features and service advantages over previously available technologies.

- SMR is an example of a mobile system that has gained significantly as a result of switching to digital technologies.

Tell Me More

Digital wireless technologies provide a platform for new features, including many of those long available to more traditional wireline telecom service users. Perhaps even more important, digital makes more efficient use of the radio frequency spectrum. With the analog cellular spectrum largely exhausted, wireless carriers have turned to digital networks to take up the slack and add capacity to cover their rapid subscriber growth.

Digital technologies have also played a key role in the development of Specialized Mobile Radio (SMR) dispatch services for commercial business users. The introduction of Integrated Digital Enhanced Network (iDEN), which provides digital mobile phones with messaging capabilities and the ability to simultaneously communicate with up to one hundred people, has been a key factor in SMR growth.

Future developments, such as the eventual rollout of third-generation (3G) cellular systems, will significantly add to the features and benefits of personal mobile communications.

7.6 How do I evaluate a digital mobile service?

There are basically four very important issues to consider when selecting a digital wireless service. Known in the industry as the Four C's, they are clarity, cost, coverage, and capacity. Each of these elements is extremely important in selecting a mobile phone and service.

- *Clarity.* Voice clarity can vary noticeably from one digital technology to another.

- *Cost.* New and competitive services have helped drive prices down on both phones and service.

■ **Coverage.** Coverage is particularly important in rural areas or where different service plans are being offered.

■ **Capacity.** All digital networks offer more channel capacity than analog services, and some digital systems offer more channel space than others.

Tell Me More

The criteria for evaluating a digital service should cover clarity, cost, coverage, and capacity.

Clarity. Although generalizations can be made about the relative quality of any of the major digital wireless systems, field trials by service providers and surveys by analysts indicate that voice clarity can vary noticeably from one digital technology and mobile phone to another. With subscribers consistently ranking voice quality high on surveys, wireless carriers have worked hard to improve and promote the quality of their service. Some carriers have resorted to free trials to allow consumers to test the quality of their service. Unfortunately, few new wireless subscribers actually test phones with an actual phone call before purchasing it. Most subscribers who are upgrading their phone and/or service rely on experience, product reviews, and word of mouth before making a new mobile phone purchase.

Cost. Users don't have to look at many advertisements to realize that pricing plans vary widely and are often confusing. In fact, the introduction of new digital services, such as PCS, in some regions of the United States has helped drive cellular service prices down and has made wireless services generally more competitive with basic wireline telephone service. This is particularly true for businesses that buy a "bulk" wireless telecom service plan.

Coverage. In terms of coverage, the selection of a service provider usually requires a little more homework by the subscriber because of the differences in the "footprint" (literally, the geographic area of coverage of the wireless network) held by regional and national wireless carriers.

Selecting a cellular or PCS carrier and then a service plan should be based on personal requirements, such as minutes used, range of travel, and the availability of features (an answering service, for example).

Where many of these systems start to get complicated is with the availability of dual-mode (analog and digital) and dual-band (phones that operate in two different radio frequencies) handsets.

Dual-mode phones are necessary (at least in the United States) because some regions of the country still do not offer digital service. However, the entire United States is analog-enabled. This means that if you have a dual-mode phone, you can use it anywhere in the country. If digital service is not available, or if it's the wrong digital service, the phone will automatically and seamlessly switch to the analog mode.

Capacity. Capacity remains a vague issue for the mobile device owner. However, all digital cellular services offer more transmission capacity than analog service, mainly in the form of more channels, which means that more voice and/or data traffic can be transmitted over a digital network. Although this is transparent to most mobile subscribers, it is important from the standpoint of knowing that service is available and a big improvement over the still-active analog network. As an economic or technical issue, network capacity is very important to a network operator as they add subscribers and new services.

7.7 What are the transmission speeds of wireless networks?

Selecting the right mobile device requires that you know what you're going to do with it, and that usually means determining what key features you need. One of those features is the data transmission speed. How much data will you need for your application and how fast do you have to send it or receive it?

Tell Me More

In terms of end user services, data rates are important. So-called first generation (1G) cellular phones—all of which were analog models—operated in the 1 kilobit per second (kbps) range and, other than voice communications, could only display text information. Second generation (2G) cellular models operate at 28.8 kbps and offer graphics, e-mail, Wireless Application Protocol (WAP) browser functionality, in addition to text and voice service. Enhancements to 2G digital services have pushed data rates to another level known as 2.5G, with data rates mainly in the 64 to 144 kbps range.

The next generation, or third generation (3G), cellular service will operate initially from 384 kbps for mobile and 2 megabyte per second (mbps) for fixed applications, but eventually will climb into the 8 mbps data transmission speed range, and will add several new services, including video and audio streaming, and digital pictures. Currently, the advertised data rates for wireless networks don't exceed 9.6 kbps. However, in actual use, these networks usually perform at slower speeds. At some point, 3G is expected to be able to transmit digital data at significantly higher speeds than the 2 mbps that will be available initially.

Here is a simple guide to the major wireless systems and their data rates:

TODAY'S SYSTEMS

Motient (formerly ARDIS)	19.2/4 kbps	Packet
CDMA	N/A	N/A
CDPD	19.2 kbps	Packet
Cellular (analog)	14.4/9.6 kbps	Dial up
GSM	9.6 kbps	Dial up
BellSouth Mobile Data	8.9 kbps	Packet

TOMORROW'S NETWORK SPEEDS

Motient (formerly ARDIS)	28.8 kbps	Packet
CDMA	28.8 kbps	Circuit/Packet
CDPD	28.8 kbps	Packet
Cellular	28.8 kbps	Circuit/Packet

GSM	14.4 kbps	Circuit/Packet
BellSouth Mobile Data	9.2/28.8 kbps	Packet

Source: www.wireless.com.

* Dial up usually refers to using the public switched telephone system to make a call on a dial or pushbutton phone (as opposed to an upgraded or high-speed service, such as DSL or cable modem, etc.). In the case of cellular, the process is the same but the wireless network is used to "dial up" a call.

7.8 What does international roaming mean?

Roaming, the ability to use a wireless phone to make and receive calls in places outside of one's home calling area, has expanded to international mobile communications services, with network operators entering into roaming agreements with foreign wireless service providers, or carriers. These agreements enable a mobile subscriber in one country to communicate with a subscriber in another country (using that country's network).

The roaming agreement between the two operators allows them to transfer call charge data and subscription information back and forth as their subscribers roam into and out of other networks.

- Subscribers can reach each other by mobile phone throughout Europe because network operators in each country have signed reciprocal roaming agreements.

- In addition to voice, international roaming is also available for e-mail, Internet, and fax services.

- Network operators with roaming agreements normally exchange subscriber data.

Tell Me More

In a typical international roaming scenario, a subscriber in the United Kingdom can use his phone when traveling to Spain. This is possible because his home operator has a roaming agreement with a network operator in Spain.

While in Spain, the subscriber can make voice calls and can also be reached by anyone who dials his home number. The subscriber will also be able to use e-mail, browse the Internet, send and receive faxes, and securely access a local-area network or intranet, provided that both the home network and the visited network support these services.

When the subscriber returns to the United Kingdom, the bill from his home network operator will include all his mobile phone usage in Spain because all the billing information will have been transferred to his home operator.

7.9 What are the most prominent digital mobile technologies?

There are several digital mobile technologies. They include:

- General Packet Radio Services (GPRS)

- Enhanced Data for GSM Efficiency (EDGE)

- High Speed Circuit-Switched Data (HSCSD)

- International Mobile Telecommunications-2000 (IMT-2000)

- Universal Mobile Telecommunications System (UMTS)

- Wideband CDMA (WCDMA)

Tell Me More

General Packet Radio Services. General Packet Radio Services (GPRS) is an extension of the GSM standard that includes packet data services. It is a packet-based data standard 2.5G technology developed for existing high-speed data transmission. GPRS offers a minimum speed of 9.6 kilobits per second (kbps), with the promise of future data transmission speeds of 115 to 160 kbps. GPRS uses a packet switching technique, which means that it uses the network only when there is data to be sent. Today's circuit-switched technology, on the other hand, establishes a dedicated and uninterrupted connection between the sender and receiver. Circuit-switching is used in standard telephone service. The launch of GPRS service in the United States is scheduled for mid- to late 2001.

Enhanced Data for GSM Efficiency. Enhanced Data for GSM Efficiency (EDGE), developed by BellSouth, is also a data-based technology that gives GSM and TDMA similar capacity to handle services for 3G mobile communications. EDGE was developed to enable the transmission of large amounts of data at a high speed, 384 kbps, for the first phase of 3G deployment.

Although EDGE depends on GPRS equipment to provide services, it is not necessary for a wireless network operator to offer GPRS before providing EDGE services. EDGE has been approved as a technical standard by the European Telecommunications Standards Institute (ETSI).

High Speed Circuit-Switched Data. High Speed Circuit-Switched Data (HSCSD) is a multislot (multichannel) data transmission technique for GSM networks. As a multislot data transmission technology, the transmission can simultaneously use up to four time slots in a channel for data. This means files can be downloaded faster, with faster wireless Internet and e-mail access.

Based on the GSM voice protocol developed in Europe, HSCSD has been standardized by ETSI. HSCSD-equipped phones are currently available and transmit at 14.4 kbps over a single channel (or slot); however, HSCSD will ultimately enable much greater data speeds of up to 57.6 kbps in GSM networks. Launched in September 1999, HSCSD was implemented by GSM operators globally for their networks as an interim step toward the adoption of 3G.

International Mobile Telecommunications-2000. International Mobile Telecommunications-2000 (IMT-2000) is the basis for which the 3G standard was developed and approved in June 2000 by members of the Geneva-based International Telecommunications Union (ITU), an arm of the United Nations. IMT-2000 has been in development for more than fifteen years.

Universal Mobile Telecommunications System. Universal Mobile Telecommunications System (UMTS) is the European mobile cellular standard for 3G. UMTS is based on IMT-2000 and it supports broadband services, such as voice, data (including Internet access), and multimedia. The UMTS data rate varies by application. It is 144 kbps for vehicular use, 384 kbps for pedestrians, and 2 mbps for fixed (usually in-building) applications. Licenses for UMTS have already been awarded to network operators in several countries in Europe and Asia.

Wideband CDMA. Wideband CDMA (WCDMA) is supported in the United States by Voicestream and Cingular Wireless, both of which use GSM digital networks. Both wireless carriers are upgrading their networks to support GPRS, EDGE, and WCDMA.

In addition to making very efficient use of the available radio spectrum, it features data-transmission rates of 5 MHz or higher with multimedia access at up to 2 mbps in a local area and 384 kbps for wide-area access, meaning that it can serve a campus-type environment or operate through a network that uses local telephone company lines to connect geographically dispersed sites. WCDMA service is expected to be available in 2004.

Cdma2000 technology was developed out of cdmaOne, which has similar capabilities but is actually second generation (2G) cellular data technology. One version of cdma2000 is known as cdma2000 3X because it needs three times as much spectrum to operate as cdmaOne. However, the wireless carriers that have committed to cdmaOne believe they can offer 3G speeds on their networks with a variant called 1X. Sprint PCS, Verizon Wireless, and Qwest Wireless have deployed cdmaOne, mainly for field testing. It was developed by Qualcomm and approved as a technical standard by the Telecommunications Industry Association in conjunction with the Third Generation Partnership Project 2 (3GPP2).

Chapter 8

Location-Based Services

8.1 What are location-based services?

Mobile location services enable location-specific information and applications to be delivered to mobile handsets. Services include telematics (vehicle tracking, traffic reports, maps and directions), leisure activities (helping to locate parks or restaurants), and entertainment (locating movie theatres, concert halls, etc.).

- There is no uniform technology standard for location-based services.

- Location-based technologies give advertisers a whole new outlook on impulse buying.

- Detailed travel information is now available from a mobile device.

- Access to location-based information will be available from a variety of products in different form factors, from handheld devices to wristwatches.

■ Tracking and monitoring large fleets of vehicles by satellite has become a huge business.

■ Location-based personal profiling information raises privacy concerns.

Tell Me More

The interoperability of mobile systems and networks that might be applied to location-based services could become an issue as consumers and network operators are faced with a variety of position-location technology choices, including AOA (angle of arrival), Cell-ID, E-OTD (enhanced observed time difference), GPS (Global Positioning System), A-GPS (assisted GPS), D-GPS (differential GPS), signal attenuation, and TDOA (time difference of arrival).

Location-based technology offers fantastic opportunities for advertisers. For example, since you know where people are, you can promote impulse buying through offers and advertisements for nearby businesses. Even more exciting are the opportunities that arise from using both location-based technology and personal profile information in tandem to target advertising to specific individuals, which could work like this: As your vehicle approaches a Chinese restaurant, which you have already identified as a favorite type of cuisine, your on-board system acknowledges its specific location and sends you a message that it is offering a one-day special on scallops with black bean sauce.

On a more portable level, there are companies such as Vindigo (www.vindigo.com) that provide custom travel information for PDA owners in nineteen U.S. cities (see Question 6.1). Users register on the company's Website and download software onto the desktop personal computers. After installing Vindigo's software on a Palm or Handspring device, you can automatically enter updated information into the Palm by synchronizing with your desktop PC. PDA users can find directions to just about any location or address through the PDA's GPS module.

Motorola has also formed an alliance with MapInfo Corp. to provide MapInfo's miGuide, a location-based application that delivers maps and driving directions, and which allows you to check Yellow Pages and retail business locations on wireless handsets. Similarly, Trimble, a GPS specialist, has formed Trimble Information Services to offer Internet location-based services for the mobile workplace by offering complete end-to-end fleet management services.

Much more highly miniaturized products are also under development, including wearable personal location devices, designed into a wristwatch, which help consumers determine the location of their children, elderly parents, or other potentially at-risk persons.

Tracking and Monitoring. Tracking and monitoring large commercial trucks by satellite has become a significant development in the past several years because trucking companies have accepted technology as a major productivity enhancement tool.

The most successful of these systems is Qualcomm's OmniTRACS mobile communications system. Today, more than 1,250 trucking fleets in the United States are using OmniTRACS to communicate with drivers, monitor en route vehicle location, and collect other valuable real-time vehicle data, such as the status of refrigerated trucks. More than 370,000 OmniTRACS units are operating in the United States, Japan, and Europe, using either the Global Positioning System (GPS) or Qualcomm's proprietary satellite positioning system.

OmniTRACS is a data-only system that can communicate around the clock between its network control centers in San Diego and Las Vegas and trucks traveling across the country. In actual use, the network control centers can pinpoint the location of a specific truck right down to an intersection. The trucks are equipped with special satellite antennas located outside and above the cab of the truck. The driver has access to a full-text, keyboard-equipped terminal to send and receive messages, including routing information (or rerouting if a scheduled stop has been cancelled), weather and road data, specific directions to each scheduled stop, and personal information (such as "call home at your next stop").

OmniTRACS features include:

- Real-time data communications

- Automatic vehicle tracking

- Seamless, nationwide coverage

- Data integration capabilities

- Route planning

OmniTRACS can also be used to track untethered trailers and railroad cars, and to monitor the status of refrigerated trailers and rail cars.

Privacy Concerns. The use of information from wireless sources to reduce traffic congestion, speed response teams to roadway emergencies, and assist drivers to find the most efficient routes using in-vehicle navigation is subject to much debate.

Rapidly developing technologies can gather and synthesize information in real time, but many of the legal ramifications of information gathering are not well understood, although some effort is being made to address these issues.

Clearly, consumers are concerned about how this information might be used. Fifty-six percent of the people recently surveyed by The Yankee Group said they are somewhat or greatly worried about the threat of how such information might be used, while 64 percent were somewhat or greatly worried about personal profiling on their mobile devices.

The Intelligent Transportation Society of America (ITS America) promotes the use of information technology in surface transportation to save lives, time, and money, and to improve the quality of life. But concerns about how the technology might be used has promoted the organization to publish *Privacy Principles*, which specify that intelligent transportation systems should conform to several rules or ideals. These include recognizing and respecting the individual's interests in privacy and information use, and complying with state and federal laws governing privacy and information use.

8.2 Are any other satellite-based navigation systems in development?

The European Union (EU) has embarked on the very ambitious Galileo program, a satellite network that is designed to handle virtually all of Europe's civil navigation requirements.

■ The new European navigational satellite system and Russia's GLONASS network are technically compatible.

■ Galileo will use medium-earth-orbit (MEO) satellites.

Tell Me More

Europeans have for some time been concerned about having to rely on a satellite-based navigation system that is owned and operated by the U.S. Department of Defense (DOD), and they have been developing their own system for several years. Although not scheduled to be operational until 2008, the system, known as Galileo, is a result of the formation in 1991 of the European Geostationary Navigation Overlay Service (EGNOS), which operates independently of, but is compatible with the DOD-operated Global Positioning System (GPS) and Russia's Global Navigation Satellite System (GLONASS).

GPS and GLONASS each feature twenty-four orbiting satellites, although it is rare that all of the GLONASS satellites are operating at the same time. Galileo will be made up of either nine geostationary satellites and twenty-one medium-earth-orbit (MEO) satellites, or thirty MEO satellites, orbiting the earth at an altitude of 1800 miles. These are essentially the same orbit altitudes used by the United States and Russians, but they will be optimized to cover Europe. Geostationary means that the satellites are always over the same location of the earth. Medium-earth-orbit refers to their distance from the earth when in orbit.

8.3 What is the status of communication satellites?

Very high expectations but low user interest have plagued the mobile communications satellite field almost from the day these systems were proposed.

■ Mobile communications satellite systems designed to provide voice and/or data services have had major problems getting their low-earth-orbit (LEO) satellites into service.

■ Until very recently, satellite services found it difficult to build a revenue-generating subscriber base. The September 11, 2001 terrorist attacks on New York City and the Pentagon have changed that.

Tell Me More

Mobile satcom service is currently available in many parts of the world from Iridium and Globalstar, but both companies have experienced highly publicized difficulties in signing on enough subscribers to support their business. Mobile communications satellite systems designed to provide voice and/or data services, such as Iridium, Globalstar, ICO Global Communications, Teledesic, and ORBCOMM, have had major problems getting their low-earth-orbit (LEO) satellites—those operating at 420 nautical miles above the earth—off the ground and into service.

Subscribers to each of these services use handheld phones, similar to cellular phones, but much more expensive and slightly larger and heavier. The big difference between cellphones and the new mobile satellite phones is that the satcom devices can make and receive calls to and from virtually anywhere in the world. The service, initially at eight dollars and higher per minute, has been significantly reduced to, in some instances, less than a dollar a minute.

Iridium initially targeted corporate and government VIP users as well as underdeveloped and developing countries with limited telecommunications resources. Created several years ago by Motorola, Iridium began operating in November 1998 and actually terminated service in March 2000. Iridium has since regrouped under new management as Iridium Satellite LLC, offering voice and limited data service in the United States. It also has developed a new business plan, focusing on customers who need mobile telecom services in remote areas, such as maritime, construction, forestry, emergency services, and the military.

Globalstar L.P., a consortium led by Loral Space and Communications and Qualcomm, has continued to provide data, video, and high-speed two-way Internet access to consumers via a 48-satellite network, but at one point suspended indefinitely its principal and interest payments on all of its funded debt, citing high costs and the difficulty of raising funds from investors. Loral says its plans now call for simply providing satellite capacity to projects in fast-growing market segments like transportation and government services.

Like Iridium, Globalstar has been developing a new business plan, focusing on niche commercial markets very similar to those being pursued by Iridium.

Another entrant in what is considered to be an already crowded field is ICO Global Communications, headed by Craig McCaw, who sold McCaw Cellular to AT&T (now AT&T Wireless) for $11 billion. ICO Global plans to focus on niche markets, such as shipping and trucking. Scheduled to launch its service in 2003, the company also has a new identity—New ICO. Current plans call for it to market special devices that attach to existing portable phones rather than developing totally new and more costly dedicated phones for its service.

Yet another and perhaps the most ambitious mobile satellite service is Teledesic. Created and largely financed by Microsoft's Bill Gates and Craig McCaw, Teledesic is a global, 840-satellite network designed to provide mainly high-speed data and Internet access beginning in 2005. McCaw has suggested that at some point ICO and Teledesic might merge into a full-service, and presumably more competitively priced, mobile satellite service provider, to be called ICO-Teledesic.

More recently, New ICO Global Communications asked the Federal Communications Commission (FCC) to allow it to develop land-based cellular services using radio spectrum normally reserved for satellite communications. The proposal is aimed at getting around one of the problems currently facing Iridium and other mobile satcom providers; that is, providing reliable satellite communications from inside buildings and in urban areas with tall buildings. ICO believes that a network of strategically placed land-based towers would solve this problem and make ICO more closely resemble a cellular network.

Another mobile satellite system is ORBCOMM, which provides data-only LEO two-way monitoring, tracking and messaging services to more than 40,000 mobile terminals throughout the world. Most of ORBCOMM's business comes from tracking mobile assets, such as trailers, containers, locomotives, rail cards, heavy equipment, fishing vessels, and barges; monitoring of fixed assets, such as electric utility meters, oil and gas storage tanks, and wells and pipelines; and messaging services for consumers and for commercial and government users.

In February 2001, ORBCOMM announced that it was seeking bankruptcy court approval to begin an auction to sell the business while it was still in operation. ORBCOMM operated under Chapter 11 bankruptcy proceedings from September 2000 and was acquired by International Licensees LLC in April 2001. International Licensees is a consortium of ORBCOMM licensees and other investors established by Gene Song, chairman of ORBCOMM Asia Ltd. and ORBCOMM Korea Ltd., and Don Franco, chairman of SATCOMM International Group Ltd., a major shareholder in ORBCOMM's European licensee.

Efforts to market mobile satellite phones have proved difficult from the beginning, mainly because the phones and their "air time" are more expensive than cellular phones. However, the sale of handheld Iridium and Globalstar phones jumped significantly following the terrorist attacks on New York City's World Trade Center and the Pentagon, when cellphone network traffic reached the point where people could not make calls for hours. Following the events of September 11, 2001, several government agencies and a number of global business organizations decided to acquire mobile satellite phones, thus providing the services with an unexpected boost in revenue.

8.4 How do these mobile satellite systems work?

Each satellite system works a little differently, which helps explain why they require a different number of satellites. Briefly, for example, the Iridium phone will communicate directly with the closest satellite before linking to a terrestrial communications network. Globalstar's dual-mode handsets seamlessly switch from conventional cellular telephony to satellite services.

- The ORBCOMM system sends a message from a handset to the satellite. It is then relayed to one of four U.S. gateway earth stations.

- There are other satellite systems in Asia and Europe.

Tell Me More

Iridium is a network of sixty-six satellites. It was originally conceived as a system of seventy-seven satellites—hence, the name Iridium for the element whose atom has seventy-seven orbiting electrons. Motorola engineers were able to reduce the number of satellites in the system to sixty-six and still cover the entire earth. Each of these satellites will orbit about 420 nautical miles above the earth.

When Iridium subscribers initiate a call, the nearest satellite in the system automatically identifies the caller account and the location of the user. If the subscriber's local cellular system is unavailable, the Iridium phone will communicate directly with the closest satellite. The call will be switched from satellite to satellite through the network to its destination—either another Iridium phone or an Iridium ground station, which can complete the call through the local, land-based cellular network infrastructure.

The Globalstar system is fully integrated with existing fixed and cellular phone networks. Using a different system architecture than the other mobile satellite services that requires only forty-eight orbiting satellites, Globalstar's dual-mode (satellite and cellular) handsets seamlessly (and transparently to the user) switch from conventional cellular telephony to satellite services.

In the data-only ORBCOMM system, a message is sent from a remote subscriber handset in the United States—either a stationary or mobile unit—and is received at the satellite. It is then relayed to one of four U.S. gateway earth stations. The gateway then sends the message via satellite link or dedicated landline to a network control center, which routes the message to the final addressee via e-mail, dedicated telephone line, or facsimile. Messages originated outside the United States are routed through gateway control centers in the same manner.

Outside the United States, the Indonesia-based Asia Cellular Satellite System, known as AceS, made its debut in late 2000. AceS serves only Asian countries, including Taiwan, Korea, India, Thailand, and the Philippines. Subscriber rates for this system, which uses a dedicated portable phone and a single geostationary satellite, are much cheaper than for Iridium or Globalstar.

Paris-based EUTELSAT expects to launch e-Bird, a new satellite optimized for Internet access, in the second quarter of 2002.

8.5 What is the future of satellite radio broadcasting?

By the end of 2001, two new satellite services—XM Satellite Radio and Sirius Satellite Radio—will offer digital-quality, commercial-free broadcasts of music, news, and sports programming on up to one hundred stations, twenty-four hours a day, throughout the United States.

The two companies are using the entire spectrum allotted to this service by the Federal Communications Commission, which the FCC has formally designated Satellite Digital Audio Radio Service.

- XM Satellite and Sirius Satellite have lined up several consumer electronics manufacturers to build their radios.

- The two companies will charge a monthly fee of approximately ten dollars to access their service.

- XM and Sirius also plan to use terrestrial transmitters to fill in gaps where their satellite signals may not reach, such as in cities with tall buildings.

Tell Me More

Both companies have lined up several manufacturers to produce their mobile radios, which are expected to be priced in the $200 to $300 range. Also, hoping to give radio the kind of boost that cable gave television, the two companies will charge a monthly fee of approximately ten dollars for their service. As a result, the radios will require a conditional access system, such as those used in the cable TV pay-per-view system. The service providers must encode the content (music, news, etc.) before it can be broadcast. Also, several major national retailers, including Radio Shack, have agreed to merchandise these systems to consumers.

One of the unique advantages of this service is that anyone, particularly long-haul truck drivers, can drive from coast to coast without changing the station or losing the signal. XM Satellite will use two geostationary satellites for its network, while Sirius Satellite has three geosatellites in orbit.

In addition to their satellite operation, both companies will use terrestrial transmitters to fill in the gaps where satellite signals might not reach, such as cities with tall buildings, mountainous regions, and other areas with similar obstructions.

8.6 What is telematics?

Telematics is a set of technologies that combines wireless voice and data communications with the Global Positioning System (GPS) satellite navigation system to deliver information, location-specific security, and productivity-enhancing services to road-based vehicles.

These systems usually require an in-vehicle computer and are connected wirelessly to a central service center.

- The systems perform a variety of safety and work-related functions.

- In-vehicle position-location/navigation is a key element of many telematic systems.

- General Motors' OnStar is currently the most widely deployed telematics system in the United States.

- Voice recognition is expected to make using telematic systems both easier and safer.

- In-vehicle navigation systems are very popular in Tokyo, where street addresses are not sequential.

- The European Telecommunications Standards Institute has drafted a technical standard for location-based mobile systems.

Tell Me More

Today, telematics systems offer drivers emergency and roadside assistance, in-vehicle navigation, remote door unlock (if you lose your keys or lock them in the vehicle), stolen vehicle tracking services; they can also instantly notify a central tracking office when an air bag deploys.

Some of the features available through turn-by-turn navigation systems, such as iRadio, a joint product development effort by Motorola and Navigation Technologies, include:

■ *Web-based trip planning,* enabling drivers to create a personal profile of addresses, trips and preferences that can be downloaded prior to entering the vehicle.

■ *Point-of-interest searching,* enabling users to easily find favorite restaurants, gas stations, museums, stores, shopping centers, and theatres. Categories and names can be preprogrammed into a personal profile via the system's Web site.

■ *Personal information management,* which enables the system to synchronize with Microsoft Outlook and similar software, as well as Palm-type devices, to allow users to access their address book, calendar, or other personal information and to navigate to addresses and appointments. This feature also enables users to create route markers that function very much like bookmarks on the Internet, allowing drivers to return to locations of interest.

■ *Hands-free capabilities,* including voice recognition, text-to-speech capabilities, voice maneuver prompting, and real-time traffic and weather information.

■ *Infrared (IR) beaming,* which operates like a TV remote control device, gives the user the ability to "beam in" a destination address by pointing an IR-equipped cellphone or Palm-type devices at an in-dash IR receiver.

One of the most popular telematics systems currently in use is General Motors' OnStar, which GM launched in 1996 on three Cadillac models. The service uses a GPS satellite network and cellular technology to link drivers and vehicles to a call center with live operators. For the 2001 model year, OnStar is available on thirty-two of fifty-four GM vehicles, either as factory-installed standard equipment or as part of an option package. OnStar had nearly 800,000 subscribers at the end of 2000 and is adding more than 4,000 new subscribers a day.

Each automotive company determines its own pricing, but telematics systems currently range from $500 to $2,000 in North America and

Europe. Some top-of-the-line GM vehicles include the OnStar system at no additional equipment charge, but they require a monthly service fee, which varies depending on the level of service provided.

Surfing the Web while driving may seem dangerous; however, the use of voice recognition and voice synthesis technologies for hands-free operation for most telematic functions is expected to make using these systems both easy and safe. (Advanced Recognition Technologies has also developed voice-driven applications for controlling a vehicle's lights, windshield wipers, and entertainment system, and has demonstrated a handwriting recognition technology in a pad built into the steering wheel so that only authorized drivers can start the car.)

In-vehicle navigation systems are already very popular in Japan, particularly in Tokyo where the street addresses are not sequential. NTT DoCoMo, the leading wireless carrier in Japan, is integrating a U.S.-developed commercial GPS system into its vehicle navigation and location systems. Subscribers to Japan's all-digital Personal Handyphone Service (PHS) already have access to GPS-based services, using premapped coordinates (longitude and latitude) to find their way through Tokyo and surrounding communities.

Europe also is active in developing location-based services. The European Telecommunications Standards Institute (ETSI) has drafted a technical standard for telematic services in Europe. Also, three European telecommunications companies—Cambridge Positioning System (CPS), Auselda Aed Group, and Convert Italia—have formed a consortium to offer mobile-location services in Italy using GPS technology.

One problem with all of these systems, however, is that the mapping data is usually stored on a DVD, so it is difficult to update. This is expected to change in time with the ability to transmit updated mapping data into an in-vehicle navigation or central computer system. This could be done either by communications satellites or by using the cellular network.

Ford Motor Co. has demonstrated a number of features of their telematics system at trade shows to test consumer interest. One is a video camera with a crash sensor and cellphone that transmits pictures to emergency medical services.

Ford of Europe and Vodafone Group Plc have formed a strategic partnership to provide telematic services in Europe. Their system includes voice-driven safety, security, and information services. The telematics units built into the Ford cars will use Vodafone's network services, technical capabilities and mobile phone networks in Europe. Four buttons integrated into the front panel of the stereo system in the dashboard of a Ford Focus will allow users to access the telematic system.

Mercedes-Benz is outfitting all of its cars with a GPS. The company offers its TeleAid service for drivers with in-vehicle information such as news, weather, traffic updates, and Web content.

Motorola has also developed a concept it calls the "Work Car." Its specific business applications would include synchronization with Palm-type personal digital assistants (PDAs) for out-of-office information downloads, enhanced virtual service centers, and network support "car meetings." The Work Car also features several nonbusiness functions, including real-time traffic information and remote vehicle diagnostics.

Eventually, telematics is expected to enable drivers to turn on home lights, start and stop sprinkler systems, and set their office security systems from their vehicles.

However, one of the most basic and widespread uses of tracking vehicles (and undoubtedly the most widely accepted use) will come with the emergence of Federally mandated Enhanced-911 services.

The future of telematic systems will depend on what consumers want in their vehicles. Among the possibilities are travel information (traffic updates, parking availability, airline status), messaging (voice mail and e-mail retrieval), information (sports, weather, stock market updates, and Internet access), and entertainment (audio games, books, magazines, and newspapers).

8.7 What regulations cover Enhanced-911 services?

With more than 118,000 calls a day made in the United States to 911 and other emergency numbers from wireless phones, Enhanced-911 (E-911) service, which can pinpoint the location of callers even if they do not exactly know where they are, is getting more attention. The current Federal Communications Commission (FCC) E-911 rules were adopted in 1996 and reflected the technology available at the time, which anticipated only a network-based approach, called automatic location identification (ALI). Now, with Phase I of the FCC ruling completed, emergency response centers are receiving the location of the cell tower used for incoming E-911 calls, and the FCC has shifted to its Phase II rules, which have already been revised.

- Recent developments make it possible to locate callers directly from their portable phones.

- The current approach to locating cellphone 911 callers is complicated.

- Incompatible technologies and systems have complicated efforts to easily locate people under the FCC's current edict.

- Another proposed system, not covered in the FCC's ruling, would use Web-based wireless Internet devices for 911 communications.

- Under FCC rules, E-911 services will be rolled out in phases, beginning late in 2001.

- A fully deployed E-911 system is scheduled to be in operation by December 2005.

Tell Me More

Recent technological advancements have made it possible to locate 911 callers directly from their mobile handsets, using GPS technology to determine the location of the caller within a few meters.

The current network approach requires dispatchers to use a method of triangulation to locate the caller by using radio signals from at least three cellular towers. The caller's location can be determined by measuring the signal strength the caller is closest to, then plotting the caller's distance from the other two towers. The point where all three circles of the radius of each tower intersect is the location of the caller.

To complicate the issue, wireless carriers have committed to different technologies that will allow them to locate cellphone users. Verizon

Wireless, for example, plans to adopt a network solution, while Sprint PCS has selected a GPS-based handset option. Some carriers may change their minds as FCC deadlines approach, or adopt both technical approaches.

Another carrier, SCC Communications Corp., is developing a 911 data management application using the Internet for public-safety-related calls. SCC believes that IP technology will enable the same level of service for enhanced 911 that are currently available from a desktop computer, a handheld device, a pager, or even a medical monitoring device on a wireline phone. At least half of all new phones are to be ALI-capable no later than October 1, 2001. And at least 95 percent of all new digital phones must be ALI-enabled and activated for this service no later than October 1, 2002.

The revised standards for Phase II location require carriers to achieve 100 meters accuracy for 67 percent of mobile calls and 300 meters accuracy for 95 percent of all calls. For service providers who elect to adopt the handset-based location solution (as opposed to the network-based scheme), the requirement is for 50 meters for 67 percent of calls and 150 meters for 95 percent of all calls.

The entire process is to be completed by December 2005. However, E-911 is just one of a variety of location-based services that are being developed for the mobile technology market.

8.8 What is WAAS?

Despite the proven accuracy and reliability of GPS, the Federal Aviation Administration (FAA) is developing the Wide Area Augmentation System (WAAS) to enhance the accuracy and integrity of GPS receivers.

- WAAS is a network of ground stations that monitor GPS satellites.

- WAAS offers accuracy of three meters, a big improvement over current GPS systems.

- The new system is now available for the first time for nonaviation applications, such as recreational use.

Tell Me More

WAAS consists of a network of ground stations that monitor the integrity and accuracy of GPS satellites. This information is transmitted to users via a geostationary satellite in a format that is compatible with the basic GPS signal infrastructure.

WAAS information is offered free-of-charge to GPS users and does not require the purchase of additional receiving equipment. The WAAS signal has been available since December 1999 on a near continuous basis. By using WAAS information, select GPS products can offer enhanced accuracy typically within three meters, or about five times better than most GPS products, which are not currently compatible with the WAAS system.

In August 2000, the FAA declared the WAAS available for nonaviation uses like recreational boating and camping.

Other governments are developing similar systems, such as the Japanese Multi-Functional Satellite Augmentation System (MSAS) and the European Euro Geo Stationary Overlay Program (EGNOS) system. Eventually, users around the world will have access to precise positioning, using all of these and other compatible systems.

8.9 How are telematics and location-based systems being developed and promoted?

An industry consortium, Mobile and Automotive Geographic Information Core, or MAGIC, Services Initiative, has been formed specifically to promote telematics and location-based systems. However, hundreds of companies and several trade groups have an interest in the development of telematics and location-based mobile commerce services.

- The development of location-based services may be slowed by the lack of technical standards.

- An FCC mandate for locating wireless phones in emergencies has become a stumbling block in the early deployment of location-based services.

- MAGIC is developing an open, nonproprietary industry specification for delivering navigation, telematics, and related location-based services across any wireless network or device.

Tell Me More

Location-based services are considered a compelling application for wireless service providers as well as retailers and other commercial services that hope to lure wireless device users into their establishments. However, development of these services may be slowed by the lack of technical standards. Any of these systems deployed in the 2001 to 2002 timeframe are likely to be proprietary and, therefore, they may not be compatible with other location-based systems.

Another potential stumbling block to the early deployment of location-based services is an FCC mandate that wireless carriers be able to pinpoint the location of wireless phone calls within 300 meters beginning October 1, 2001 to facilitate Enhanced-911 (E-911) emergency services. Several carriers have resisted these requirements, claiming that they cannot meet the level of accuracy required by the FCC, at least not by the FCC's deadline.

The MAGIC initiative, and those of other groups interested in promoting location-based services, are aimed at delivering high-performance, low-cost geographic data services to laptop and handheld computers, personal digital assistants (PDAs), mobile handsets, in-vehicle positioning systems, and other mobile devices. MAGIC services will support basic geographic operations needed by almost every mobile application. These functions include:

- *Geocoding.* The conversion of text or speech defining an address or location to corresponding geographic coordinates (latitude and longitude)

- *Reverse Geocoding.* The conversion of geographic coordinates to an address expressed either as text or speech

- *Spatial Query.* Calculation of the distance to or travel time remaining to reach a position, region, or route based on current location

■ *Travel Planning and Guidance.* The specification of travel destinations and intermediate waypoints as well as the location and time-sensitive delivery of information and instructions to en route travelers

MAGIC is open to a wide range of industries and partners, including navigation data content vendors, navigation and telematics system developers, telematics service providers, wireless carriers, and application developers.

In addition to MAGIC, an international group of eight companies formed the Wireless Location Industry Association in December 2000 to promote the public acceptance of location-based technologies and applications.

8.10 What mobile services are available for travelers?

Online mobile travel services have been available for some time, although they vary in capability and features.

■ Airline Web sites accounted for 58 percent of online bookings in 2000, but few of these were made on mobile devices.

■ Several travel-specific online Web sites now offer wireless-enabled systems for booking flights via mobile devices.

Tell Me More

PhoCusWright, a travel research organization, estimates that airline Web sites accounted for 58 percent of online bookings in 2000, a jump from 53 percent in 1999. The number of tickets purchased via mobile devices is believed to be quite small so far. Even though there are currently few products and services available to book travel and check the status of flights and other forms of transportation, this is likely to change over the next two to five years.

Air Canada is working with IBM to develop a Web-based wireless tracking system. The airline says that it expects to save $130 million on IT costs over seven years and enhance its revenue by offering the developed technology to third parties. Initially, the service will eliminate lines by enabling agents to come to the customer and print out boarding passes. Eventually, the service will allow customers and the airline to track luggage through a Web interface.

Currently, one of the relatively few services available for purchasing tickets directly from an airline is United Airlines' United.com. The level of service varies with the type of wireless device you're using to access the system. Generally, however, United.com offers wireless booking and ticketing. Also, flight status, flight availability, flight paging, upgrade status, and access to a summary of a Mileage Plus account are available on Palm devices and Wireless Application Protocol (WAP)-equipped mobile phones and pagers. The United site cannot rebook flights.

United Airlines has also announced one-time paging registration for customers requesting mobile alerts about flight changes. This feature is now part of United's previously announced Proactive Paging service, which enables customers to check itineraries, flight status, and seat assignments.

Alaska Airlines provides flight schedules, flight status reports, a wireless check-in service, and frequent flyer account information to business travelers via Web-enabled cellphones and PDAs.

Singapore Airlines (SIA) has launched its SIA Flight Status and SIA Flight Alert mobile services to NTT DoCoMo's i-mode mobile phone subscribers in Japan. The services enable SIA customers to obtain information using mobile phones, PDAs, and PCs. The services have a global user base of 25,000 subscribers.

Lufthansa has made it easier to board flights in Germany with the introduction of its m-Barq system, developed with Siemens Business Systems. Using a cellular phone, Lufthansa's e-ticketed customers can check in at an interactive kiosk. The e-ticket is delivered directly to the customer's WAP-enabled phone, transmitted in the form of a barcode instead of a ticket number. Upon arrival at a Lufthansa kiosk in the airport, the customers simply waves the phone over the scanner (just like checking out groceries), answers some security questions, and receives a printed boarding card.

Sabre Holdings Corp., a specialist in travel-related technologies, is working with Motorola to deliver wireless services to business travelers via Motorola's Mobile Office product. Using Sabre's wireless travel services and Mobile Office, business travelers can access updated travel information through any WAP/HTML-enabled wireless device. At any time, travelers will be able to:

- Receive alerts for fight delays, cancellations, and gate changes as well as receive trip reminder information

- Access time schedules, flight numbers, gate numbers, weather conditions, and other general flight information

- Create reservations for airlines, hotels, or car rentals

- View or cancel existing travel reservations

Sabre Holdings has also partnered with BlueTags—a Danish company that develops radio frequency identification (RFID) tags for handling, detecting, and monitoring objects—to develop eBaggage for tracking luggage. Based on Bluetooth and RFID technologies, the wireless bag tag enables users to detect and identify their bags when entering and leaving predefined area, check bags faster, and track bags via wireless or Web-enabled devices. Users of the tag simply download their entire travel itinerary to the tag and attach it to any bag. Travelers can electronically check their bags with the airline by using special scanners. Upon arrival, travelers receive messages on their Web-enabled mobile phones or other wireless devices, providing information about the location of their bags.

Mobile device owners can also book flight, car rental, and hotel reservations on Travelocity.com. Travelocity.com users can also rebook flights on its mobile phone channel with service through AT&T Wireless, British Telecom, Nextel Communications, and Vodafone, and on wireless PDAs via Omnisky and Palm. Travelocity.com can display flight information and weather. Travelocity.com is also the content provider for Yahoo! Travel (travel.yahoo.com) for dial-up Web-access cellphones in the United States, and for Sprint PCS Internet-ready phones.

The Sprint PCS/Travelocity.com arrangement includes Sabre Holdings, a technology and marketing services provider for the travel industry. Most travel agents use the Sabre system to book flight reservation. The agreement links the Sabre Virtually There Web site (www.virtual-lythere.com) to the Sprint PCS wireless Web. This allows Sprint PCS customers who have booked their travel through a Sabre-connected travel consultant to access to their Virtually There travel itineraries, including flight details, gate information, and weather forecasts via their Sprint wireless phone. The service enables Sprint PCS customers to book flights for almost any airline and even rebook an existing flight to an earlier or later time.

So far, trips can only be booked or rebooked online for cancelled or delayed flights through Trip.com.

I-tinerary, a specialist in business travel, has been set up to automatically alert mobile phones, pagers, Palm PDA, and Pocket PC of users who subscribe to the service about trip delays, flight cancellations, and other data. It can also suggest and book alternate flights, and notify rental car agencies and hotels of flight delays. Another service, Everypath, offers flight schedules and flight status information, as well as mileage plan reports from airlines that participate in the program.

Clearly, some adjustments may have to be made in these systems and procedures following the terrorist attacks on New York City and the Pentagon. Also, with the airlines cutting back on flights, laying off personnel, and adding security, it may take longer than anticipated to roll out these wireless technologies. On the other hand, these events may actually speed the development of wireless technologies in security applications.

8.11 How is mobile telemetry being used today?

Wireless telemetry is used to transmit data for the purpose of remotely monitoring sensors of any type (temperature gauges, counters, flow meters, on/off switches, etc.) from a distant location.

- Telemetry is being used to remotely read utility meters and vending machines.

- A primary application of telemetry is for medical devices.

Tell Me More

Wireless telemetry technology can transmit data from monitoring devices like thermometers at a distant weather station or a flow meter on a gas line from remote locations. It can also check on the inventory status of a vending machine to avoid an unnecessary service call. Currently, most applications for portable telemetry products are used for asset tracking, inventory control, and medical assistance.

Several vendors have linked navigation and position location, using the satellite-based Global Positioning System (GPS), to track and monitor truck fleets. The system also sets off an alarm and transmits a vehicle's position if it is stolen or tampered with. Since the system is two-way, a central monitoring center can shut down the engine and lock the doors. Of course, automobile racing has been using telemetry for years to monitor everything from critical engine conditions to tire pressure.

Although most remote monitoring is done by landline or satellites, digital, cellular, and two-way paging have opened up new opportunities for low-cost mobile telemetry.

Some mobile equipment vendors and network carriers have developed telemetry as a niche business. For others, it is their core business.

Remote Equipment Monitoring. Some two-way paging carriers have formed telemetry business units for everything from monitoring the status of photocopiers and vending machines in areas where wireless connectivity is necessary or preferred. Isochron Data Corp., for example, has partnered with WebLink Wireless and Motorola to enable vending machine operators to remotely monitor the inventory of their automated ice machines located outside grocery and convenience stores.

Utility Meter Readers. Utility companies have started using one of the analog channels of cellular networks to access and read utility meters.

Medical Assistance. Medical telemetry devices are being used as heart monitors, and to keep track of medical equipment that is moved around hospitals on carts.

Data Critical Corp., has also introduced a wireless telemedicine central computer for storing and distributing key files that transmits patient data, including electrocardiogram (ECG) waveforms. In addition, Data Critical can transmit patient-monitor data to a handheld Nokia 9000i Communicator, a combination cellular phone and PDA.

Comsearch, an Allen Telecom Co., for example, has been selected by the American Society of Healthcare Engineering (ASHE) of the American Hospital Association (AHA) as their technical partner to perform frequency coordination services in the new Wireless Medical Telemetry Service (WMTS). In response to growing concern for interference resulting from new digital television transmitters, low power TV transmitters, and greater use of Private Land Mobile Radio equipment, the Federal Communications Commission (FCC) established the WMTS. This service has three dedicated assigned frequencies—608–614 MHz, 1395–1400 MHz, and 1429–1432 MHz—that are used for the interference-free operation of medical telemetry systems in hospitals.

In this capacity, ASHE is responsible for overseeing and managing the WMTS spectrum usage to ensure interference-free operation and electromagnetic compatibility (EMC) between medical telemetry devices. All transmitters operating in the WMTS bands must be registered with ASHE to ensure interference-free operation.

Wireless telemetry is also being used to help save energy. Aeris.net, a provider of Web-to-wireless machine-to-machine communications services, has initiated a service in California that enables machines—such as heating, ventilation, and air conditioning (HVAC) equipment, boilers, pumps, holding tanks, and other devices—to be remotely managed and monitored through secure communications over cellular networks so that a user with a PC or server on the Internet can make energy-use decisions based on incoming data.

The Yankee Group has predicted that the number of wireless telemetry units in service will grow by more than 500 percent through 2005, especially in such business sectors as atmospheric control, health care, municipal services, security, transportation, and utilities.

Chapter 9

Mobile Commerce Applications

9.1 Where do shopping and other retail services fit into mobile commerce?

Online shopping is one of the most lauded elements of mobile commerce (m-commerce). However, despite very high expectations by many industry leaders and analysts, this sector has been very slow to develop. One reason for this is that a common infrastructure has not been available to enable wireless shopping on any kind of noteworthy scale. Another is that consumers have shown little awareness or interest in shopping in a mobile environment.

- Consumers aren't likely to buy big-ticket items using their cellphones, but efforts are underway to promote and optimize wireless shopping.

- Personalized, location-based services are just beginning to emerge for Web-based mobile devices.

- America Online (AOL), Microsoft, Yahoo!, and Yada Yada are likely to offer the most strongly featured location-based, interactive shopping systems.

- Increasingly, companies are using mobile commerce techniques to improve efficiencies in their business operations.

Tell Me More

Although it is unlikely that anyone would use their cellular phone, pager, or personal digital assistant (PDA) to buy big-ticket items such as cars or furniture, several efforts are underway to optimize wireless shopping for mobile device users on a more practical scale.

One obvious example of using mobile devices in a retail environment (and one that is already in use) is mall-based auto repair shops issuing pagers to customers who can shop until they are beeped that their vehicles are ready for pick up. But that's purely a customer service feature. The big push is for personalized, revenue-generating location-based services.

In one possible scenario, a consumer would hear a new song she liked and would then log on to Amazon.com or a similar site using a Web-enabled mobile phone or PDA, and then purchase the CD. In a technically more sophisticated scenario, passing a Burger King would trigger an audible signal on a cellphone or PDA and display the Burger King logo. The device's display would show the specific location of the fast-food restaurant, and offer a two-for-one coupon, or a free drink, good only for that day.

Yada Yada, an integrated wireless Internet service provider, is working with three companies in an effort to make the wireless shopping experience easier. They are:

- DealTime (www.dealtime.com), a leading online comparison-shopping service

- BarPoint.com (www.barpoint.com), a product information service

- SNAZ Commerce Solutions (www.snaz.com), a global wireless commerce provider that features a "single-click" Web shopping destination

Yahoo's mobile network, Yahoo Everywhere (mobile.yahoo.com), has added location-based information for wireless phone users. Consumers with Web-based mobile phones can type in their location and obtain local travel, entertainment, restaurant, and other information.

Using another service, Yahoo Local Info, consumers can choose from a list of favorite locations, find addresses, check distances, get directions, and access local businesses and services.

Other major players, such as America Online and Microsoft, are developing similar, or more strongly featured, m-commerce capabilities. Indeed, AOL's acquisition of Time Warner is expected to lead to the promotion and sales, through the AOL portal, of magazine subscriptions, music, videos, and other products and services. Microsoft has partnered with Nextel Communications to introduce MSN Mobile 2.0, a wireless information service for Web-enabled cell phones with access to MSN Hotmail, MSN MoneyCentral, Expedia, MSNBC, and other Web-based content, including door-to-door driving directions and MSN Yellow Pages.

Some current examples of mobile retail/shopping services are:

- Guests of the Holiday Inn on Wall Street in New York City can check in and out of the hotel, access their rooms, and pay for meals at the hotel's restaurant by using a Bluetooth-enabled cellphone for short-range data exchange.

- Starwood Hotels & Resorts Worldwide, whose guests include mostly business professionals, has tested Bluetooth in some of its hotels to provide similar services.

- Peachtree Networks has introduced an online mobile grocery shopping service. The system operates through wireless carriers in the United States and Canada. Retailers take orders from mobile phone users and deliver groceries. So far, however, the service has not gained much interest. Most consumers who have logged on to the service have done so to check weekly specials and access discount coupons, but they continue to physically shop the stores.

- Several professional sports teams, such as the National Hockey League's Carolina Hurricanes, offer tickets wirelessly to promote impulse ticket purchases. Part of the Hurricanes' marketing strategy includes a five dollar discount for tickets purchased using a mobile device.

■ T.G.I. Friday's global restaurant chain offers a restaurant locator and its menu via Internet-enabled mobile phones and wireless handheld devices. If a business traveler from Boston is in Orlando, she can click the "Auto Locator" to display the distance in miles, street address, and a phone and fax number for the nearest Friday's restaurant. The locations of T.G.I. Friday's restaurants in fifty-three countries are available from Friday's wireless site.

■ The Ritz Group is using a personalized e-mail (www.ritzcamera.com) campaign to target 200,000 customers who have already made purchases at Ritz stores. If a customer has purchased a digital camera, for example, the e-mail would recommend an auxiliary lens or other accessories for the camera.

Another example of m-commerce service is available from FedEx and UPS, which can track their customers' packages from wireless devices. FedEx customers can find addresses, directions, and drop-off times by zip code on their wireless device, using a special interface device.

9.2 Will wireless advertising work?

Sending very brief advertisements to mobile devices—such as cellular phones, pagers, and PDAs—owned by highly targeted subscribers is already underway, but has met with mixed reviews. Although some market analysts believe that these "micro ads"—mainly banners, logos, and e-mail messages—are too small to be very effective, a growing number of potential advertisers are taking them seriously.

■ Surveys indicate that consumers will accept advertisements sent to their mobile devices if they receive something free in return.

■ Ericsson has teamed with a Canadian advertising agency to test wireless advertising late in 2001.

- The Newspaper Association of America is conducting a pilot program to determine how best to make news and other information, including advertising, available to mobile device users.

- One of the challenges facing mobile device designers is how to display useful information on tiny screens.

Tell Me More

Several wireless advertising programs are already well underway. However, one of the obvious questions about wireless advertising is, does anyone want these services? Several surveys indicate that most consumers will accept push technology—that is, advertising that is sent to them without their having specifically requested it—if they receive something free in exchange, such as a phone, free service, or discount coupons for merchandise. However, a market study in late 2000 by Jupiter Media Metrix indicates that advertisers will probably be slow to spend money on this type of advertising. When someone figures out how to measure and show the benefits of advertising on these devices, no doubt things will change dramatically.

According to Jupiter, to maximize ad campaigns on these devices, advertisers must match the marketing message to the objectives of the consumer using the device—not to their demographic profiles. Jupiter believes that ad opportunities for mobile devices are in the need-to-have category for a few advertisers and only nice-to-have for most advertisers.

As with most surveys done by others, Jupiter found that many consumers were willing to accept advertising on their mobile phone or PDA with subsidized content and access, or a subsidized device. For example, Burger King might offer a free drink with any order to anyone who allows the fast-food chain to display its logo from time to time on their wireless device. However, nearly half of all the users surveyed said that no form of compensation would persuade them to receive advertising on their mobile phone or PDA.

An Ericsson-sponsored study indicates that mobile users are not only receptive to ads delivered to their phones, but they will respond to them as well. The Ericsson study, conducted in Sweden, sent 100,000 messages over a six-week period. The volunteer users completed a demographic profile questionnaire and received ads targeting their demographic group—a completely different approach from the one recommended by Jupiter Metrix Media, and one that may have been designed to generate more positive results. Ericsson has teamed with Profilium, a wireless content provider, and Cossette Communications, Canada's largest ad agency, to test location-based wireless advertising. The test is scheduled for late 2001.

Analysts believe recent studies of consumers' reaction to wireless advertising have profound implications for wireless carriers who are looking for any competitive advantage and opportunity to differentiate their services.

Carriers are also looking for ways to generate revenue from these services; for example, by sharing in the income from ticket sales for sporting events and concerts promoted by the carriers to their subscribers. They also believe there is a perception that advertising adds value to the carrier's WAP service by providing what amounts to a new information "alert" service, with the potential to add more advanced location-based mobile commerce services in the future. Carriers also see wireless advertising and other forms of wireless promotion as an opportunity to help them retain subscribers with a regular diet of new service and product announcements and promotions.

In February 2001, the Newspaper Association of America and Aether Systems, which develops mobile messaging and data products and services, launched a pilot project aimed at helping newspapers determine how best to serve their mobile readers with news and information, including advertising.

The project initially hopes to establish a "local news gateway"—a central index hosted at Aether's network operations center in Owings Mills, Maryland—through which users can access content from multiple participating newspapers via phones and PDAs. Using the gateway, the NAA and participating newspapers will explore how mobile users access news, weather, sports, and other information as well as wireless advertising. Participating newspapers will track which sections of their wireless news sites are accessed most often and when, enabling them to determine what type of content is most valuable to consumers on a wireless platform.

One of the challenges in wireless advertising is how to develop very short but effective ad messages for these tiny, monochrome, cellphone and pager displays? Another issue, and one that will require some experimentation and study, is how to measure consumers' response to wireless ads. For example, do they "click through" to a ticket service after seeing an ad for an upcoming jazz concert? Using current and fast-emerging next-generation technologies, how can wireless carriers count how many people responded to a wireless ad and therefore make a case for others to use this new service?

Given the hundreds of millions of cellphone and other mobile device users worldwide, wireless advertising is viewed as a very attractive opportunity by ad agencies and their clients. The Yankee Group is projecting a $6 billion wireless ad market by the end of 2005.

9.3 What types of wireless advertising exist?

Wireless advertising is in the very early stages of development, and its effectiveness will depend on how it is accepted by mobile device owners. There are various types of advertising available.

- SkyGo tracks and analyzes click-through, ad recall, and user feedback for advertising directed toward mobile devices.

- General Motors' OnStar has been experimenting with location-based advertising.

Tell Me More

SkyGo, formed in 1999 to provide technology for wireless interactive marketing, tracks and analyzes click-through, ad recall, and user feedback for advertising directed toward mobile devices. They have identified several key types of wireless device advertising, including:

- *Interactive branding.* These messages employ two-way communication to engage the consumer in trivia, instant surveys, games, and polls to foster an awareness of specific brands of products and services, and to reinforce these messages.

■ *Sales alerts.* These time-sensitive updates provide information on sales and special offers targeted to consumer interests and demographics. They may also be used for location-based services in the future.

■ *Coupons.* These alerts that provide a coupon the consumer can redeem, driving traffic to brick and mortar stores.

■ *Incentive ads.* These messages offer consumers an incentive to buy in the form of a gift or promotion with purchase.

■ *Audio ads.* These messages contain links to audio samples, recorded information, interviews, and music selections.

In addition, SkyGo is experimenting with advertising that includes specific "calls to action." They are currently delivering and tracking consumer response to ads that enable:

■ *Click to buy.* These alerts contain a one-click "Buy Me" option, encouraging the consumer to make a purchase via m-commerce.

■ *Click to e-mail.* One click allows the consumer to send additional information to an e-mail inbox.

■ *Click to visit WAP site.* One click takes the consumer to an advertiser's WAP site.

■ *Click to call.* One button activates voice services, connecting the consumer directly to the advertiser, enabling him to buy over the phone or ask for more information.

General Motors' OnStar has been experimenting with location-based advertising that would be sent to vehicles via the OnStar network. Drivers willing to receive promotional voice messages on specific topics would have to complete a questionnaire detailing what kind of advertisements they are willing to receive. Someone interested in golf, for example, could automatically receive a short message about a sale on golf bags at a store within two miles from the person's current location. Subscribers can also enter credit card information into an OnStar database to purchase items directly from their vehicle and then pick up the merchandise at a later time. Initially, OnStar will carry advertising from financial service providers, including Fidelity and Charles Schwab, and from sporting goods retailers. Each OnStar ad will last for four seconds.

Some other examples of wireless advertising include:

- Los Angeles-based Premium Wireless Services/Your Mobile Networks has created a database of three million wireless subscribers who have opted to receive free ring tones and commercial logos.

- PWS has been working with several movie studios, including Sony/Columbia Tristar, and other entertainment organizations, to send short messages to wireless devices promoting soon-to-be-released movies. One sample message, used by PWS to reach 60,000 mobile phone users in the United Kingdom, read: "'Final Fantasy'—Unleashed in cinemas. C more & book online with odeon@ff.co.uk.'" Another message by Universal Studios invites wireless users to visit a Web site to sign up for advance information on the release of "Jurassic Park II," with the chance to win a trip for two to Costa Rica.

9.4 How can wireless advertising be sent to mobile users without invading their privacy?

Privacy is a major issue among advertisers and mobile network carriers. One of the key concerns is how to deal with spam or push advertising, which is advertising or other types of promotional messages that has not been requested by the mobile subscriber.

In 2000, privacy moved to the forefront with negative publicity after a major Internet advertising specialist became the subject of a federal investigation for trying to merge anonymous online customer data with personal offline information.

- Studies have been conducted to determine how mobile users would react to ads sent to their mobile devices.

- The Wireless Advertising Association (WAA) has created a set of privacy guidelines for sending ads to mobile devices.

- The WAA has established "confirmed opt-in" promotions as the de facto standard for wireless advertising.

- One of the concerns about location-based services is that wireless service providers may track wireless subscribers' location.

- The introduction of digital imaging will extend wireless advertising to still images and full-motion video.

- Legislation banning wireless advertising has been introduced by Representative Rush Holt (New Jersey), but has not received wide industry support.

- The Cellular Telecommunications and Internet Association (CTIA), a trade association that lobbies the U.S. Congress and federal regulators for its wireless carrier member companies, has been working on its own location-based privacy guidelines and intends to use them to lobby against further regulation with federal agencies.

Tell Me More

Several studies have been conducted to assess subscribers' privacy concerns and how they would react to mobile ads. As a result, the wireless advertisers have worked together to create guidelines for protecting the privacy of individual wireless users. One of the first acts of the Wireless Advertising Association (www.wirelessadassociation.org) was to recommend privacy guidelines for its members. The WAA is an independent strategic organization unit of the Internet Advertising Bureau, which promotes and monitors advertising on the Internet. These guidelines are aimed at setting acceptable standards for using personally identifiable information (PII), marketing, and mobile e-commerce in the wireless medium.

The WAA's basic position is that wireless advertising should only be sent to individuals who want it. In other words, wireless subscribers should control their PII. PII is defined as data that can be a name, address, phone number, and e-mail address. Non–PII data is not uniquely and reliably linked to a particular person, including but not limited to activity on a wireless network, such as location or log files related to

Web browsing on a mobile device. For example, your name and your credit card number are PII, but the fact that twenty people checked out a new movie on the Web is not PII information.

The WAA, formed in May 2000, also declared that "confirmed opt-in" promotions should be the de facto standard for wireless advertising. A *confirmed opt-in* is defined as a process of verifying a subscriber's permission to receive wireless ads in order to ensure that push messaging and/or content is not accidentally or maliciously sent to the subscriber's wireless mobile device. A standard opt-in requires an active choice by the wireless subscriber.

Adopting some of the guidelines of the Online Privacy Alliance, the Network Advertising Alliance, and the Internet Advertising Bureau, the WAA has produced the following voluntary principles:

- WAA members should adopt a privacy policy regarding PII that is readily available to consumers at the time that PII is collected and should encourage business partners to do the same.

- WAA members should notify wireless subscribers of how PII is being used.

- WAA members should give users notice and choice regarding the use of PII, and they should not use PII for purposes other than those for which it was collected without explicit consent. Such consent shall be obtained by confirmed opt-in.

- The WAA does not condone wireless spam.

- WAA members shall make every effort to ensure that PII is accurate and secure, and, where reasonable and appropriate, shall allow wireless subscribers access to correct or delete such information.

One of the concerns about location-based services is that wireless service providers may pinpoint the location and virtually track wireless subscribers who don't "opt in" to this feature. There is also the matter of unresolved federal standards and regulations, and the WAA says it intends to work with mobile network carriers on an ongoing basis, as well as with direct marketers and their industry associations.

Legislation that bans wireless advertising has been introduced by Representative Rush Holt (New Jersey). However, the legislation has not received strong support from either the wireless industry or anti-spam crusaders. Several pieces of legislation have also been introduced in Congress to protect privacy when using cellular phones. One of them is the Know Your Caller Act (H.R. 90), which protects consumers who subscribe to Caller ID services. Currently, telemarketers can block their identities from being transmitted through Caller ID. The Know Your Caller Act would end that practice. Another proposal is the Online Privacy Protection Act (H.R. 89), which requires Web sites to notify Web visitors that personal information is being collected from them. The Wireless Privacy Protection Act (H.R. 260) protects consumers from having their wireless service providers track their location.

The CTIA has been developing its own set of wireless privacy policies and plans to promote its position to the Federal Communications Commission and Federal Trade Commission.

Few wireless marketers claim to have a real sense of what will work or what is acceptable to the mobile consumer. For the moment, the opt-in approach is believed to be the best way to go—at least until more advanced and sophisticated techniques are tested and developed.

9.5 Can mobile communications be used to conduct market surveys?

Some independent market research organizations and wireless interactive marketing firms are already using Web-based wireless phones and PDAs to conduct consumer surveys.

- Surveys conducted by mobile devices usually generate a high response and faster results than more traditional polling methods.

- Wireless surveys can reach thousands of people in a niche market group.

- Client companies are concerned about the accuracy of these surveys.

Tell Me More

Consumer surveys using mobile devices provide a high response rate and faster results than more traditional market research methods. A recent example is SkyGo's survey of how consumers react to wireless advertisements on mobile phones. The survey began in September 2000, when SkyGo delivered wireless ads to study participants in Boulder, CO, who opted to receive a minimum of three daily "alerts." SkyGo tracked, compared, and analyzed click-through and action rates, ad recall, and user feedback until the trial concluded on January 31, 2001.

Other companies that have conducted marketing surveys using wireless devices include Japan's NTT DoCoMo, which used its i-mode system of online services with more than 20 million subscribers to conduct short surveys, and Europe-based Wireless Opinion, which send out questionnaires using the Short Message Service (SMS).

For marketers, the plus side is that once you have developed your database and your system is up and operating, you can send thousands of e-mail messages to niche demographic groups fairly inexpensively and very quickly.

There is a downside, however. As analysts who have begun to use the Internet to conduct online market research have discovered, these surveys are not always accurate. The wireless users who are willing to participate in a survey represent a certain type of person. Their opinions cannot be assumed to reflect those of the general public.

Another concern is that online survey groups do not generate the type of subtle information that often comes out of face-to-face sessions in that it is not possible to respond to others' nonverbal cues or body language.

Also, wireless Web-based surveys tend to have a high development cost, making them relatively expensive for small-sample polling.

9.6 Is the financial industry going to offer mobile commerce programs to its customers?

Mobile payments and related financial services are expected to become an important part of the bank-consumer relationship over the next four to five years. The Mobey Forum has been formed to encourage the use of mobile technologies in financial services.

- Advances in mobile technologies are redefining the point of sale in North America.

- Mobile product and service vendors are working closely with financial services organizations to develop and deliver financial services via the mobile Internet.

Tell Me More

Advances in mobile technologies and the growing population of mobile workers is redefining the point of sale in North America and other parts of the world. Several financial services vendors and others have recognized this trend and are developing a wireless payment strategy.

- *VeriFone,* a division of Hewlett Packard, for example, has formed a joint venture with Palm to develop and promote their secure payment systems on Palm wireless-enabled handheld devices.

- *IVI Checkmate Corp.* has signed an agreement with GTE Wireless Solutions whereby IVI Checkmate will supply wireless terminals for financial services applications through GTE Wireless' national Wireless Retailer Program.

- *Registry Magic,* which develops biometric access security systems, such as retina scanners and palm print readers, is working with major cell phone manufacturers, wireless carriers, and credit card companies to help launch its Consumer Payment Network. For the wireless payment system to work, participating retailers will need to attach a wireless adapter module to the back of cash registers. Then, consumers with Bluetooth-enabled phones will be able to make wireless payments at those registers.

Here's how it works: Consumers indicate to the cashier that they want to use their phone to make a purchase. The cashier rings up the sale. The phone then beeps and displays a message to enter a PIN number, and "speaks" a previously recorded code word. To enhance security, the user's picture appears on the cash register screen. The phone then offers a menu of billing choices to the user to complete the transaction.

A survey of attendees at the 2001 National Restaurant Association Show indicated that more restaurateurs and food-service personnel are considering obtaining the technology they need to run their businesses via the Internet, including the use of wireless technologies. Wireless applications, which would allow managers to receive alerts—via cellphones, PDAs, and other Wireless Application Protocol (WAP)-enabled devices—and Web-based reporting were ranked high among the capabilities that were considered useful by the show's attendees. Specifically, access to real time information was the most desired capability sought by restaurant and food-service managers.

Another development is the use of dedicated, or store-specific, smart cards to attract and retain customers. Starbucks Coffee, working with Microsoft, will begin field-testing a system in late 2001 that allows subscribers to pay for their coffee and other products using their personal wireless devices and a Starbucks smart card. The card will activate the mobile device, which links to wall-mounted wireless transceivers in participating Starbucks stores, and then bill the customer later.

In addition to the efforts of the Mobey Forum (see Question 9.7), there are also agreements between industry companies aimed at developing new business models for themselves and their customers in creating mobile Internet-based financial services.

One such agreement is between Ericsson and IBM. The two companies are working together to help financial services companies deliver mobile Internet offerings, such as the retrieval of checking account information. They are focusing their efforts on high-volume business-to-client services, such as wealth management, account aggregation, mobile trading, and credit card, and payment alerts.

When their agreement was announced, a joint statement by IBM and Ericsson about their project said, "While many benefits have been realized, financial services companies now are faced with the challenge of delivering higher-value financial services to hundreds of thousands of customers located around the globe." IBM and Ericsson expect to develop the infrastructure that will integrate the mobile Internet into the business strategies of financial services companies. If successful, the existence of the infrastructure is expected to accelerate the acceptance of the mobile Internet for financial services and help drive the development of additional applications and traffic.

Another effort is underway from Euronet Worldwide, which provides secure financial transaction solutions, and Stet Hellas Telecommunications S.A., a Greek mobile network operator. The companies have teamed up to offer mobile banking to financial institutions in Greece, such as banks, credit unions, brokerages, and mutual fund companies. Stet Hellas and Euronet will offer Short Messaging Service (SMS) and Wireless Application Protocol (WAP)-based account access and event messaging services.

9.7 What is the Mobey Forum?

The Mobey Forum (pronounced Mo-bay) has been formed to encourage the use of mobile technologies in financial services, including wireless payment and remote banking and brokerage services. One of its most important tasks will be to promote and help develop global technical standards for financial services for wireless Web-enabled devices.

- Forum members include some of the largest and most well-known banks in the world.

Tell Me More

The Mobey Forum (www.mobeyforum.org) was founded in August 2000 by a number of banks and mobile device manufacturers. The forum's central goal is to encourage the development and deployment of financial services over the wireless Web.

The forum believes that consumers will eventually use mobile handsets as payment devices, but that this will require a secure infrastructure before it can attain full market acceptance.

Nokia, Motorola, and Ericsson were invited to join the Mobey Forum to work with the banking and financial communities to develop and implement these requirements.

The forum's founding members include ABN AMRO Bank, Banco Santander Central Hispano, BNP Paribas, Barclays Bank, Deutsche Bank,

HSBC Holdings, Nordea, SEB-Skandinvaviska Enskilda Banken, UBS, Visa International, Ericsson, Motorola, and Nokia. New members include Credit Suisse, BBVA (Banco Bilbao Vizcaya Argentaria), the Information and Communications Mobile Group of Siemens AG, DBS (Development Bank of Singapore), Bank of Ireland, Svenska Handelsbanken, and Credit Agricole. Among its associate members are the Wireless Information Network, Industry Wed Networks, Proton World, Earthport, Lucent Technologies, Andersen Consulting, Baltimore Technologies, Noblestar, and Entrust Technologies.

Chapter 10

Security and Privacy Issues

10.1 What security and privacy issues should mobile device users be concerned about?

Security threats to mobile devices from hackers and other sources have become a problem, albeit, a slowly growing one, and they are beginning to receive more press and media coverage.

- The growth of mobile communications traffic could lead to more sophisticated viruses targeting mobile devices.

- The results of a study by the American Management Association on how companies intercept employee e-mail could lead to tracking of employees' mobile communications.

- Although three levels of security have been designed into Bluetooth, at least three types of "potential vulnerabilities" have been found in the technology by Bell Labs scientists.

Tell Me More

One of the primary concerns among security professionals is that the rapid growth of mobile communications will lead to more sophisticated viruses designed to target wireless systems. Security specialists have already warned that hackers can intercept data on Palm-type PDAs. There was also a widely-publicized virus that targeted the Palm PDA.

A survey published late in 2000 by the American Management Association reported that 38.1 percent of major U.S. companies intercept employee e-mail, a significant increase over the 14.9 percent reported in 1997. Although not specifically directed at users of mobile products and services, the survey raises questions about how wireless systems users will be treated in the corporate environment. In that connection it is noteworthy that a research team at the University of California at Berkeley discovered a vulnerability in GSM phones that would enable hackers to eavesdrop on conversations.

Security is part of the fundamental architecture of Bluetooth, the short-range (up to ten meters) wireless technology developed as a cable replacement for interconnecting cellphones, PDAs, laptop computers, and many other mobile devices.

The Bluetooth community says it is confident that the technology is as secure as its applications require. But with literally hundreds of millions of Bluetooth-enabled devices expected to be in use worldwide by 2005, and because of the complexity of the technology, some analysts believe that Bluetooth devices could be vulnerable to security attacks from hackers. Another concern is how corporate IT departments can adopt and integrate Bluetooth into their current security systems and policies.

In the fall of 2000, scientists at Bell Laboratories discovered "potential vulnerabilities" in the security of Version 1.0B of the Bluetooth standard. One of the vulnerabilities opened up the system to an attack in which an adversary under certain circumstances could determine the key (part of the cryptographic algorithm in the system) exchanged by two victim devices, making eavesdropping and impersonation possible. This can be done by exhaustively searching all possible personal identification numbers (PINs), but without giving yourself away by interacting with the victim devices.

The Bell Labs scientists suggested several alterations to fix the security problems, which they believe can be implemented without major modifications.

In terms of privacy, the emergence of location-based technologies could, for example, beam unwanted messages to consumers' mobile devices based on their predetermined shopping habits.

10.2 What is the U.S. Government doing to address privacy concerns?

The response to security threats has taken several forms, including the introduction of several bills in the U.S. Congress.

- Privacy law proposals are before the U.S. Congress and state legislatures.

Tell Me More

At least three online privacy laws were before the U.S. Congress at the beginning of 2001, and trade groups estimated that more than 300 online privacy laws would be introduced at the state level during 2001.

Meanwhile, the U.S. Federal Trade Commission has indicated that it will regulate Internet Web sites against deceptive business practices, and it has already ruled in a consent decree against a Web site for allegedly violating consumer privacy rights. The FTC has already ruled that consumers must be notified of a Web site's privacy and data collection practices.

10.3 What is wireless fraud?

Cloning cellular phones or stealing users' phone numbers to make free phone calls is probably the oldest and simplest example of wireless fraud. With technology advances, education, and law enforcement, cloning is not as serious as it used to be. But it is worth monitoring.

Other concerns—not exactly in the wireless fraud category but of growing concern to the developers and users of mobile technologies—are hackers and viruses. With the extraordinary growth of wireless communications, some hackers are turning their attention to wireless networks and, in a few remote cases, have added viruses to the system. This is not a major issue at this time, but it concerns IT managers, particularly those with little experience with mobile technologies, or those who are planning to ramp up their corporate mobile technology programs.

- Most fraudulent wireless calls occur when a phone is reprogrammed with a counterfeit account code.

- Federal laws are now in place to discourage wireless fraud.

- FCC rules prohibit tampering with the electronic serial number (ESN) inside a wireless phone.

Tell Me More

There are a number of ways to make fraudulent calls, but essentially the technique consists of taking apart a wireless phone and reprogramming it with a counterfeit account code. This tricks a wireless system into sending the bill elsewhere.

Since the customer should not be stuck with the bill, virtually every wireless service provider has a policy that removes fraudulent charges from the accounts of customers. However, wireless fraud is not a victimless crime. It adds to the service providers' cost of doing business, and legitimate customers are inconvenienced since they must change their number when their phones are reprogrammed.

Although most of the problem is found in the big cities, wireless fraud can take place anywhere. Specifically, it is a violation of federal law (Title 18, Section 1029) to knowingly and with intent to defraud, use, produce, or traffic in one or more counterfeit wireless phones. On October 24, 1994, President Clinton signed the Communications Assistance for Law Enforcement Act (H.R. 4922) into law. Amendments to that law now also cover the fraudulent alteration of telecommunications equipment.

Meanwhile, the U.S. Senate has enacted legislation (the Wireless Telephone Protection Act) to strengthen criminal penalties against wireless phone cloners.

The rules and regulations of the Federal Communications Commission (FCC) also prohibit tampering with or altering the electronic serial number (ESN) inside a wireless phone. Every wireless phone must have a unique ESN ID number embedded in its circuitry, and no two phones may have or emit the same ESN, according to FCC rules.

In the past, some cellular carriers reduced fraud by requiring subscribers to use their personal identification number (PIN) before allowing access to the cellular system. This was not a popular solution because it required cellphone users to remember and enter additional numbers into their keypads. More recently, carriers have implemented various sophisticated fraud-detection technologies that help them to manage the fraud problem.

10.4 What mobile security products and services exist?

Several devices and software products are being developed to address concerns about security in mobile communications.

- New products are being developed to combat security breaches in mobile communications.

- Security devices and services include encryption, virus scans, and secure private networks.

Tell Me More

CDL-82 is an advanced encryption chip for mobile e-commerce applications. Developed by Consumer Direct Link, the chip is a trusted cryptographic component that satisfies all forms of secure financial transaction applications. It also meets Federal Information Processing Standard FIPS PUB 140-1 (Levels 2–4) requirements for strong cryptographic modules issued by the National Institute of Standards and Technology (NIST).

McAfee VirusScan Wireless is an example of a service that increases security for m-communication. It gives IT administrators the ability to scan for e-mail-borne viruses on handheld devices that run on the Palm, Microsoft PocketPC, Microsoft Windows CE, and Symbian EPOC operating systems. System administrators can install VirusScan Wireless on employees' handheld devices via e-mail. New virus definition files are updated automatically when the user connects to the Internet. The program will also scan any files transferred to or from a user's desktop computer during synchronization.

Another company, Certicom, has partnered with Cisco Systems to ensure that the system designed to request services from Certicom's virtual private network for handheld devices will work with Cisco's VPN platforms (see Question 10.11). The VPN client for handhelds also takes advantage of the company's cryptography technology to ensure secure access to internal networks for employees using wireless devices.

10.5 What are smart cards?

Smart cards, which look like credit cards, store information on a magnetic stripe or in a microprocessor chip embedded in the card. They can be used for a variety of purposes, including making phone calls.

- Intelligent cards, which is one type of smart card, stores information on a CPU.

- Memory cards are the second type of smart card.

- Smart cards are most popular in Europe, but are gaining in use in the United States.

- Subscriber identity modules (SIM cards) are used with GSM-based digital phones, mainly to accept subscription data.

Tell Me More

There are two basic types of smart cards. One is an "intelligent" card with a central processing unit, or CPU, for storing secure information. Because these cards provide a "read/write" capability, new information can be added and processed. For example, monetary value can be added and decremented as required and, as a result, these cards are considered to be more secure than other smart card technologies.

The second type of smart card is usually called a "memory" card. These are used primarily for information storage. They contain "stored value" data and could be used, for example, to ride the subway, but they cannot be used for such things as making phone calls.

Unlike in Europe, where smart cards are used almost everywhere, the use of smart cards in the United States has been limited to the availability and widespread use of older magnetic-strip credit cards. In fact, U.S. sales of smart cards are barely more than 2 percent of the industry's global total, with Europe accounting for 60 percent. But with the emergence of the wireless Web, with electronic and mobile commerce (m-commerce) expected to grow dramatically, and with the need to provide other new services requiring high security—such as banking and stock trading—normally risk-averse U.S. financial institutions are beginning to adopt highly secure chip-based smart cards.

Smart cards in the form of subscriber identity modules, or SIM cards, were introduced as part of the Global System for Mobile Communications (GSM) digital cellular standard in Europe to hold secure subscription data and applications for GSM wireless services. More than 100 SIM applications have been developed by GSM network operators around the world, including automated mobile banking and mobile trading services, location-sensitive information on demand, and roaming services.

During 2001, telecommunications industry leaders started trials of high-end GSM Java cards and Universal IC cards (which are compatible with today's SIM cards in GSM networks) for next-generation mobile phones. Among other features, the cards can be updated remotely by downloading software from wireless service providers to enhance applications with more functionality or add new applications.

10.6 How are smart cards being used today?

Most smart cards issued in the past have been dedicated to banking and health insurance. However, the growth of GSM digital cellular networks, mainly in Europe, has become a key factor in the growth and development of smart cards for telecommunications applications. These are known as subscriber identity modules, or SIM cards.

- Mobile communications are expected to have a significant impact on the development of smart cards and their use.

- Leading credit card companies are rapidly adopting smart cards and promoting their use in the United States

- Most smart cards in use today are dedicated to one industry; however multiapplication cards are in development.

Tell Me More

The impact of future smart-card developments—particularly on mobile communications networks that must accommodate much more subscription and applications data than in the past, and on portable devices such as cellular phones and PDAs—will be dramatic, especially in the United States where these cards have seen relatively little use.

MasterCard International has already sold more than 30 million smart cards in Japan, Europe, and Latin America. Visa and American Express, meanwhile, have developed their own smart card for secure online (including wireless) purchases made through their member banks in the United States. With almost 75 percent of purchase transactions globally still done using cash and checks, the credit card companies see a great opportunity in the development of smart cards. Besides ease of payment, customers using smart cards will get added value from such electronic transactions, such as purchase insurance and points of loyalty programs like air miles. Visa's branded smart card strategy includes the identification of several vertical market opportunities for developing smart-card use in wireless applications. These include fast food restaurants, automotive (including gas stations), parking garages, and pharmacies. Visa is also working with Gemplus International, a leading provider of smart cards, and Target Corp., the fourth largest general merchandise retailer in the United States, to provide smart cards and in-home smart-card readers for the Target smart-card launch. Target expects to be able to install point of sale terminals that accept chip-based payments in all its stores by the end of 2002.

The introduction of GSM digital cellular service was a major factor in bringing the smart card—in this case, in the form of a SIM card—to prominence in Europe. The use of SIMs, or similar type cards, is expected to follow worldwide. Anyone with a SIM card can use any GSM-based phone and have the call billed to them, simply by inserting the card into a slot in the GSM phone or other GSM-equipped wireless device. The network reads the SIM card subscriber's personal code embedded in the card. In fact, SIM card owners can use their cards to make calls using any phone (not necessarily their own) and the call will be billed to them.

In a mobile banking scenario, you could transfer bank funds, for example, by inserting a SIM card with your personal ID and other subscriber data into its slot in a cellphone or PDA. Using the keyboard to access your account, you would then follow a sequence of instructions displayed on the screen of your mobile device.

Today, there are more than 430 million SIM cards in circulation worldwide, but only 8 million were in use in the United States at the end of 2000.

Nextel Communications' iDEN/GSM900 i2000 phone also uses a SIM card to retrieve numeric assignment module (NAM) information previously stored in the phone. Motorola's i3000 will also require SIM cards for regular wireless service.

Glempus International has developed with Qualcomm, a leading U.S. wireless technology provider, a SIM card and a portable phone that is compatible with GSM and the Qualcomm-developed CDMA (code division multiple access) digital cellular system. CDMA system subscribers traveling to countries using different networks, such as GSM, can remove the SIM card and plug it into a CDMA-based handset for immediate access to the new network.

Microsoft has also announced plans to provide SIM smart cards to mobile network operators that deploy mobile commerce applications based on the Windows platform and applications for Windows. Windows Powered Smart Cards enable developers to design smart cards for a variety of applications.

Multiapplication Cards. Most smart cards issued in the past have been dedicated to banking, health insurance, or other information requiring a high level of security. Mobile commerce also requires security, but its biggest role will be in driving the development and widespread use of smart cards for a variety of business and consumer-oriented applications.

Industry leaders are now saying that they expect strong demand for high-end mobile applications and multiapplication smart cards. Several of these cards have already been developed and introduced. Fujitsu Ltd., for example, is promoting its ferro-electric random-access-memory (FRAM) technology for multiapplication use in mobile phones and other wireless devices. By inserting these cards into a specially-designed slot in mobile devices, users would have access to banking and ticketing services, medical information, and other mobile communications applications. Fujitsu says it expects the market for these cards to climb to 8 billion units worldwide by 2005.

10.7 Are smart cards secure?

Security in the mobile network is one of the big selling points for smart cards, particularly for people who believe that a wireless system is less secure than more traditional wired networks.

Anticipating the development of many new applications, various expert groups have been formed within industry forums to promote technical specifications for wireless security. The Smart Card Alliance's Digital Security Initiative (DSI) has, for example, launched the Case Study Report Project to create a dossier of successful smart-card-based digital network security programs. The objective is to provide senior business managers with information that enables them to justify and implement smart-card-based digital security systems.

- A critical concern about smart card use is security, but it could also be one of their biggest selling points.

Tell Me More

The DSI Expert Committee believes that a lack of understanding has caused many organizations to miss an opportunity to vastly improve the security of their digital networks through the use of smart cards. The case study report will be a collection of actual implementation experiences, and it is intended to address as many types of security applications as possible across a wide variety of industries. Meanwhile, Glemplus has teamed with Nokia, Sonera, and Omnitel to test in a series of field trials the secure payment of wireless Internet services using a Wireless Application Protocol (WAP) Identify Module in a GSM SIM card.

One recent development aimed at meeting growing consumer demand for improved security and greater storage capacity for data, video, and audio files is the introduction of a 128-megabyte Secure Digital (SD) Memory Card by Toshiba America Electronic Components Inc. Designed for use in wireless and portable communications devices—including PDAs, cellular phones, handheld PCs, digital still and video cameras, MP3 players, car navigation systems, and electronic books—the Toshiba card stores up to four hours of music or forty minutes of video. Toshiba says its new card is designed to accommodate a broader range of applications requiring greater amounts of secure file storage. Its features include cryptographic security, improved protection of copyrighted data, a high data transfer rate for fast copy/download, and high storage capacity. The new SD Memory Card meets specifications defined by the Secure Digital Association.

10.8 What are RFID-enabled cash payments?

Radio frequency identification (RFID) is another fast-growing wireless application that is finding wide use in security, access control, trans-portation, assembly-line management, asset tracking, animal tagging, and the military. Essentially, RFID devices (usually referred to as tags) send and receive an electronic signal, or signature, identifying the unique code in the RFID device. For example, RFID technology is used in several states, including New Jersey and New York, for wireless electronic toll collection by automatically identifying and billing vehicles as they pass toll stations for bridges, tunnels, and toll roads. RFID tags are also embedded in ID badges worn by employees who work in secure areas.

- There are three types of RFID tags.

- Texas Instruments has been conducting field trials of its radio fre-quency identification (RFID) technology for cashless payments in two national restaurant chains.

Tell Me More

RFID networks have certain advantages over other identification tech-nologies. Unlike bar coding, they do not require direct line-of-sight or close proximity for an identifying code to be read.

There are three types of RFID tags:

■ *Active tags* have their own internal power source, usually a battery. They can be designed to transmit at some preset interval or power up when being polled from a reader.

■ *Passive tags* have no internal power, although they may have a small internal battery to retain information in memory. Passive tags receive their power through their antenna from the reader's interrogation signals.

■ *Transponders,* the third type of RFID tag, are also passive in that they receive energy from the reader and use some of that energy to power up their circuitry and return a signal to the reader.

Texas Instruments has been conducting field trials to enable mobile-commerce cashless payments at two national fast-food restaurants using specially equipped Nokia phones. The phones contain a tiny RFID chip with a preprogrammed ID number. When customers go to the drive-through window or order their food inside the restaurant, they present their Nokia Model 5100 series mobile phones to an RFID reader and pay for their food without using cash. The system automatically bills purchases to the credit card or debit card of the customer's choice. Similar retail and banking trials are expected to develop in the next few years as financial institutions and merchants gain confidence in the technology.

Meanwhile, Texas Instruments has unveiled an ultra-high frequency (UHF) RFID technology with longer-range capability for use in very large warehouses. The new UHF reader, called Tag-it, is expected to speed throughput and boost productivity by accurately and reliably differentiating and logging fifty or more products or cartons as they pass through an inspection or assembly line.

10.9 What are PC Cards?

A PC Card is a credit card-sized device with an embedded microchip that can add functionality to wireless communications devices and portable computers in the form of new features and applications. By taking advantage of the plug-n-play flexibility of PC Cards (meaning the device's operating system has the ability to instantly recognize a card automatically without requiring the user to install special software), IT departments can easily add emerging technologies to mobile systems, thus reducing the cost of supporting corporate-standardized mobile system configurations.

- PCMCIA sets industry standards for PC Card technology.

- CardBay enables new functions to be integrated into mobile devices.

- Uses include USB-based wireless modems, security devices, and memory devices.

- Future add-on features are being considered for subsequent PC Card standard updates.

Tell Me More

Personal Computer Memory Card International Association (PCM-CIA), an international trade association founded in 1989 to establish and promote technical standards for interface cards, has released the fourth-generation standard for PC Card technology. Called CardBay, the new standard incorporates the popular Universal Serial Bus (USB) into the PC Card format widely embraced by today's mobile device developers.

Just like CardBus and the original 16-bit PC Card, CardBay enables plug-in functions to become tightly integrated within a mobile device. The CardBus standard provides higher levels of performance than the 16-bit PC Card standard. As a comparison, 32-bit CardBus cards are able to take advantage of internal bus speeds (made possible through an electrical connection) that can be as much as four to six times faster than 16-bit PC Cards. CardBus-enabled systems also support the use of virtually all 16-bit PC Cards, providing backward compatibility with the millions of 16-bit PC Cards in use today. However, CardBus PC Cards cannot be used in systems that lack CardBus slots. CardBus PC Cards employ a special keying mechanism, which prevents cards from being inserted into systems with slots that only support 16-bit PC Cards. The USB is a specification developed by the PC and telecommunications industry for connecting peripheral devices to the PC. Future extensions to CardBay are being considered for subsequent updates to the PC Card standard.

The new CardBay specification is supported by Microsoft, Compaq, Intel, Texas Instruments, 3Com, FCI Electronics, Tyco, and SCM Microsystems.

10.10 What safeguards are available against pirate wireless networks?

Pirate wireless networks are designed to "hack," or tap into, IT centers to steal corporate data. According to the Gartner Group, a telecommunications consultant and market research group, pirate wireless networks pose an increased security threat to corporations.

■ Most pirate wireless networks are jury rigged from IT department components.

■ Pirates must be within a few hundred yards from the IT network to tap into it.

■ There are several guidelines available to IT users and vendors to thwart pirate wireless network.

Tell Me More

Pirate wireless networks are usually cobbled together from components that employees have available to them in IT departments. According to the Gartner Group, to succeed in the insidious practice of tapping into secure data, wireless pirates need only to dial into the wireless network and then intercept or eavesdrop on a traditional Internet network or servers and desktop computers.

Proximity is key—wireless pirates must dial in from less than a couple of hundred yards from the traditional network they are tapping into. Gartner has developed the following set of guidelines for IT users and vendors to thwart pirate wireless network activity:

■ *Change security codes on the existing network.* Default codes are open to any third party that knows the code.

■ *Implement wireless access points.* Wireless access points are centrally located transceivers (transmitters/receivers) that provide cellular phones, wireless-enabled laptop computers, and other wireless terminals access to the local wireless network. This isolates the path that wireless users use to access your network. It also reduces the amount of backbone activity that hackers can see.

■ *Support departmental wireless networks.* Departments not totally dependent on IT support will be less susceptible to security issues.

■ *Implement Media Access Control (MAC).* MAC is the current wireless local area network standard address for controlling network security. Additionally, MAC can remotely disable wireless devices if they are stolen.

■ *Monitor access logs.* Access logs point to source addresses and make it easier to identify attempts to penetrate network log-in security.

In all cases, security efforts need to be thorough in all dimensions of the workplace.

10.11 What are virtual private networks?

A virtual private network (VPN) is a service that appears to operate as a dedicated line, but runs over the public network in a secure link over the Internet (hence, virtual private network). The major advantage of a VPN is that it is cheaper than dedicated point-to-point leased lines. VPNs are also less expensive than traditional dial-up systems for remote access to corporate computer systems. One disadvantage of VPNs is the difficulty of integrating VPN equipment into existing networks.

■ The rapid growth of mobile data traffic will require mobile professionals to easily and securely access corporate databases and applications.

- Wireless VPNs enable users of supported mobile devices to securely connect to their corporate networks and to make use of their intranet resources.

- VPNs are relatively simple for network administrators to configure and set up.

- There is a broad range of options for connecting mobile devices to VPNs.

Tell Me More

As mobile devices continue to proliferate on corporate networks and as more information is being accessed through wireless connections, the need to secure these devices has become critical. Mobile security vendor Certicom, for example, has introduced movianVPN, which lets companies securely extend their existing VPN to handheld devices that are based on the Palm OS 3.5 and Windows CE 3.0 operating systems (see Question 6.1). Future versions of movianVPN will support mobile devices with other operating systems, such as Symbian-based EPOC devices.

Many VPN gateways require simple configuration changes by the VPN administrator before the mobile device can be connected to the network. Companies that use Palm devices must set the security policy for their own employees. Several mobile devices have been successfully tested by Certicom running over IP-based services. These include mobile phones, PDAs, notebook computers, and cellular digital packet data (CDPD)-based products.

Other companies, such as Cylink Corp. and V-One Corp.—both of which have demonstrated wireless VPN products—are expected to compete with Certicom for clients who require mobile and secure access to their corporate applications on mobile devices.

Chapter 11

Electronic Payments

11.1 Who will develop electronic payments?

NACHA (National Clearing House Association) is the lead organization in developing solutions to improve the electronic payments system in the areas of Internet commerce, electronic bill payments, financial electronic data interchange, international payments, electronic checks, and employees' electronic benefits transfers.

- NACHA's focus is on developing rules and business practices.

- NACHA is working to determine whether there are any authorization issues from electronic payments in a wireless environment.

- New operating rules have been established for Internet-initiated ACH payments.

Tell Me More

NACHA's focus is on developing operating rules and business practices for the Automated Clearing House (ACH) Network, through which direct deposit payments are made. (The federal government is the single largest user of the nation's ACH, with 848 million transactions in 2000.)

NACHA represents more than 12,000 financial institutions through direct memberships and a network of regional payments associations that govern electronic payments, and 600 organizations through its six industry advisory councils. NACHA, along with the regional associations and councils, has been following the development of wireless payments to determine what, if any, electronic payments issues may arise that are unique to the mobile environment, particularly since any wireless Internet payment system would need to conform to the operating rules of the ACH Network.

11.2 What are digital signatures and why are they important?

Digital signatures are used to ensure the authenticity and integrity of documents and electronic transactions. They are based on public key encryption technology and are typically scrambled electronically during transmission in a way that the designated recipient can read it. They are also used to ensure the recipient that the digital "signature" on the document is genuine and that the document has not been subject to tampering.

- Electronic signatures now have the same validity as signed hard-copy documents.

- Digital signatures use encrypted technologies based on public key infrastructure (PKI).

- Industry analysts believe that more work may be needed to refine current legislation to ensure interoperability between systems.

- Many retailers are using an electronic box at the point-of-sale that logs a customer's signature into the store's computer when they pay by credit card.

Tell Me More

One of the more significant developments in the acceptance of electronic signatures as valid and legal in a growing number of transactions is the new Electronic Signatures in Global and National Commerce Act, signed by President Clinton in October 2000. The various provisions of the new law, known as the eSign law, take effect in steps, through 2001. Under the Act, "e-signatures" now have the same validity as a signed hardcopy document. Specifically, it states that a signature, contract, or other similar document cannot be denied "legal effect, validity or enforcement" because it is in an electronic format. Essentially, the Act gives documents with e-signatures the same legal weight as signed paper documents. However, the law does not define e-signatures because they already come in several different forms, including those based on public key infrastructure (PKI) encryption, which is used by business and government agencies primarily for signing and transmitting sensitive business contracts and other documents electronically (see Question 11.3). In practice, this technology will enable consumers to apply for business loans, sign mortgages, and conduct other business-to-business transactions from virtually anywhere.

Although it is considered a major step forward technically and a big win for electronic and mobile commerce, the Act is just that—a step forward. Most analysts in the field believe that additional work will be needed to shore up the legal language of the new law as core technologies and technical standards are identified and implemented. Further, when interoperability issues are more closely addressed, more work will be needed to ensure that electronically-based systems used for financial and other sensitive transactions are technically compatible.

Meanwhile, many department stores and other retailers have adopted digital signatures via an electronic box that customers can sign when they pay by credit card. Although all of these are currently hardwired into the store's computer, portable wireless versions of these e-signature boxes will eventually be available, mainly for use during the busy holiday season, enabling salespeople to close a sale virtually anywhere in the store. Federal Express and UPS also have people sign an electronic tablet to confirm deliveries. Legally, signed faxes are also considered to be e-signature records.

11.3 What is the Public Key Infrastructure and how does it work?

Wireless Public Key Infrastructure (PKI) provides a secure and trusted trading environment across all wired and wireless platforms by meeting the requirements of electronic security using cryptography, digital signatures, and digital certificates. These requirements include confidentiality, authentication, integrity, and nonrepudiation.

- Next-generation "personal trusted devices" will be able to conduct financial transactions on the network.

- PKI is based on a system that uses encryption algorithms for security.

- Businesses and federal agencies are already using PKI in many of their services.

- The PKI Forum was formed in 1999 to promote PKI products and services.

Tell Me More

As global mobile commerce grows, mobile devices will become smarter, evolving into what are being referred to as "personal trusted devices" that will be able to conduct secure financial transactions on any wireless network. As time goes on, security in the form of sophisticated encryption software is expected to be integrated into more mobile device operating systems and applications.

This is where PKI comes in. Essentially, PKI is a combination of software and encryption technologies that enable mainly businesses and government agencies to protect the security of their communications and electronic transactions. It is required to ensure:

- *Confidentiality*—assurance that no one can listen in

- *Authentication*—assurance that the parties you are doing business with are who they claim to be

- *Integrity*—assurance that information you send or receive is not tampered with

■ *Nonrepudiation*—assurance that agreements are legally binding

PKI is based on digital certificates, which are issued to an individual by a certification authority that vouches for the certificate holder's identity and validates the authenticity of the certificate. This must be done each time the certificate is used. The certificate contains several vital pieces of information, including the certificate holder's name, a serial number, a copy of the certificate holder's public key, the digital signature of the issuing authority, and an expiration date.

In more technical terms, PKI creates a secure environment by providing individuals with a pair of keys—a private key and a public key—through which information can be encrypted. These "key pairs" are linked mathematically using asymmetric cryptography, and each key pair is unique. The *private key* is used by the originator of a message to digitally sign the message. The digital signature is proof of that user's identity; it is the equivalent of a legal hand written signature. The corresponding *public key* is used by the recipient of the message to verify the signature. Because it is the only matching key, it is the only way the signature can be verified and provide proof that the originator of the message is who he or she claims to be, and the method by which the data is checked to ensure that it has not been changed in any way.

Some businesses and federal government agencies have been developing PKI for their services for a number of years. A study by the U.S. Postal Service estimated Government spending on PKI and related services at $2 billion. In fact, the Postal Service has been using PKI techniques since 1999, when it introduced PC Postage, enabling citizens to use their own computers to buy stamps over the Internet. More than 800,000 digital certificates were issued for that program through the middle of 2001, and the service is now being offered by commercial vendors under license to the Postal Service. However, with several U.S. government agencies using different PKI systems that do not interoperate, the Federal Bridge Certification Authority, which was set up to promote PKI interoperability, and which falls under the Federal Chief Information Officers Council, has launched a program to promote the harmonization of agency-wide PKI for use in electronic government (e-government) initiatives.

The PKI Forum was formed in December 1999 as a multivendor and end-user alliance to accelerate the adoption of PKI products and services, and to promote interoperability among PKI vendors and users. In September 2000, the PKI Forum established a reciprocal "liaison membership" agreement with the EEMA, the European Forum for Electronic Business, to help create an awareness of PKI requirements for secure electronic business across Europe and to assist vendors with PKI interoperability. The EEMA (www.eema.org), in turn, approached the European Commission for funding of a program to develop PKI interoperability testing. Called the "PKI Challenge," the program is expected to be completed early in 2003.

Many mobile transactions are already taking place. Financial institutions that need online security are among the earliest users of PKI technology (PKI is already embedded in Eurocard–MasterCards issued by its member banks), but customer relationship management (CRM) software specialists, the entertainment industry, and telecom organizations are also active in early m-commerce developments. Health care organizations are also using PKI to conform with their industry's security requirements.

Other businesses, particularly retailers and others who sell to consumers online, seem less concerned about security. However, although online purchases continue to grow, many consumers are still reluctant to send their credit card data over the Web due to a perceived lack of security.

11.4 How is wireless PKI used in a financial transaction?

A good example of how PKI works in financial transactions is Europay International, Europe's leading payment system, which provides support services to more than 9,000 member banks, and is already using wireless PKI technology.

- Wireless PKI-based transactions normally require a payment guarantee to authenticate the cardholder.

- In actual use, the PKI technology would be embedded in the mobile phone's subscriber identity module (SIM).

Tell Me More

When a Europay wireless transaction is performed by mobile phone, personal computer, or other device, a short messaging service (SMS) with the merchant's description of goods is sent to the SIM cardholder's phone. If the transaction is legitimate, the cardholder validates the purchase by sending a digital signature confirming the transaction. This provides merchants with a payment guarantee, because the signature enables the issuing bank to authenticate the cardholder and bind him or her to the transaction.

The wireless PKI technology is embedded in the mobile phone's subscriber identity module (SIM), better known as a SIM card. The SIM card stores the cardholder's "signing keys" and provides the high level of security needed for mobile payment and authentication applications.

11.5 What are manufacturers doing to make mobile financial transactions secure?

Alliances have been formed among several industry companies and organizations, and a number of technology initiatives are being pursued to enhance current security methods for mobile systems. The primary goal is to ensure that users can access and receive sensitive commercial and personal data with confidence.

- The formation of a global organization of companies is considered an important step in the development of secure wireless e-commerce standards.

- Some mobile equipment suppliers are already working to secure their products for sensitive commercial transactions.

- Ericsson and NTT DoCoMo will soon embed digital certificates into their Internet-enabled mobile phones to check the validity of financial transactions.

Tell Me More

One important effort is the formation of Radiccio, a global partnership of companies and organizations committed to the development of

secure wireless e-commerce. This effort is focused on developing standards and promoting public key infrastructure (PKI) for wireless devices
and networks.

Radiccio (www.radiccio.org) was launched in 1999, with Sonera,
SmarTrust, Gemplus, and Electronic Data Systems (EDS) as initial members. With the support of Ericsson, it has been lobbying international
organizations and government bodies to support security in global
mobile commerce, and to take mobile commerce into account when
drafting new legislation. Radiccio's members now include certification
authorities, mobile operators, system integrators, device manufacturers,
software companies, financial institutions, smart card manufacturers, and
telecom infrastructure companies.

Meanwhile, some mobile equipment vendors have already begun to
secure their products for use in sensitive commercial and personal
transactions. Both Ericsson and NTT DoCoMo, Japan's largest mobile
communications company, are beginning to use VeriSign, Inc.'s PKI technology in their mobile systems. This technology will be embedded in
Ericsson's WAP-enabled phones. For example, when a consumer uses
the phone to initiate a payment to a Web site, the phone will check the
validity of a wireless server certificate installed on a WAP server. Initially, the technology will be integrated into two Ericsson WAP-ready
mobile phones.

Japan's NTT DoCoMo will also embed digital certificates into its
phones, specifically its Java-ready 503i series mobile phones. Using the
503i phones, consumers on NTT DoCoMo's i-mode voice and Internet
services will soon be able to conduct encrypted communications with
other NTT phones and i-mode Web sites authenticated by VeriSign's
secure server ID. Using i-mode service, which was launched in Japan in
early 1999, subscribers can reserve airline and concert tickets, check
their bank balances or transfer money, and send and receive e-mail.

On another level, Nokia, Motorola, and Ericsson, which collectively
account for more than half of all cellular phone sales in the world, have
formed an organization called MeT (for Mobile electronic Transactions)
in an effort to create a common industry framework for mobile commerce, mainly in such applications as secure event ticketing, shopping,
and account-based payment services. MeT has been working to develop

core specifications and security requirements for mobile commerce. Another MeT objective is to ensure that the mobile transaction solutions that are developed worldwide are interoperable, which will ensure that consumers will have seamless access to goods and services anywhere and at anytime.

The initiative will be based on existing specifications and standards, although the founders and future members of MeT may issue additional guidelines built on emerging technologies. Any new technical developments, including any new functionality proposed by the initiative, will be submitted to standardization and specification forums/organizations, such as the WAP Forum and the Bluetooth Special Interest Group.

Examples of MeT-based transactions would include the secure use of personal credit cards, debit cards, loyalty schemes, and ticketing.

11.6 What is the impact of the terrorist attacks of September 11, 2001 on commercial privacy and security issues?

■ The terrorist attacks of September 11, 2001 have heightened the chances of employees being monitored electronically in the future.

■ Most of the technology that is needed to monitor people in the workplace is already available.

Tell Me More

Clearly, the terrorist attacks on New York City and the Pentagon have raised the specter of increased use of electronic monitoring, ranging from the use of more strategically-placed video cameras to requiring employees to carry smart cards for personal identification (complete with fingerprint and personal background data). There is also the potential for more wiretapping activity. The FBI has been trying for some time to win approval for a much wider authority to conduct wiretaps.

Code-named Carnivore, the FBI's program has been criticized by several members of Congress and privacy specialists. One concern is that the approval of Carnivore technology would make it easier for the FBI to tap into Internet service providers. It would also allow U.S. intelligence agencies to share surveillance information. Despite this and other concerns, new anti-terrorism legislation was overwhelmingly passed by Congress and signed by President Bush in late October 2001. Among other provisions, the act enables investigators to aggressively pursue suspected terrorists on the Internet.

Meanwhile, according to security experts, much of the technology that would be needed to restrict security in the workplace (instant photo ID, retina scans, etc.) is already available.

Chapter 12

Next-Generation Systems...and Beyond

12.1 What is the Third Generation?

The Third Generation (3G) is the next big step in the development of mobile communications. Third generation systems are expected to provide global access to high-speed data applications (up to forty times faster than current digital phones) for both mobile and fixed wireless services, including Internet access, multimedia, and videoconferencing with one phone or other wireless device, virtually anywhere in the world. The basic regulatory framework in the development of 3G is known as International Mobile Telecommunications-2000 (IMT-2000).

- 3G is being driven by the demand for global roaming and high-speed data transmission.

- 3G enables a broad range of advanced features and functions, one of the most significant of which is high-speed data transfer.

- Two proposed 3G technical standards are expected to prevail.

Tell Me More

The development of 3G is being driven mainly by the demand for global roaming and high-speed data transmission services. Today, hundreds of millions of mobile subscribers are using phones based on a mix of older analog and newer digital technologies.

Analog (voice only) cellular systems are known as the "First Generation" (1G) of mobile wireless technology. Today's prevailing digital technologies (GSM, CDMA, TDMA) are considered to be the "Second Generation" (2G). An interim upgrade enroute to 3G mobile systems is known as 2.5G, which embodies General Packet Radio Services (GPRS), a technology that enables wireless phones to remain "always on," meaning that users are always connected to the Internet. GPRS does not provide additional voice capacity to network operators. In fact, it reduces voice capacity when transmitting data. The minimum data transmission speed of GPRS is 9.6 kilobits per second, but speeds of 115 kbps have been demonstrated. Each of these technologies uses different data rates, applications, and products:

■ *Data Rates*

2G data rates fall into the 9.6 kilobits per second range.

2.5G data rates move up to 115 kbps (GPRS), and to Enhanced Data Rate for GSM Evolution, better known as EDGE, at 384 kbps.

3G data rates climb to 384 kbps to 2 megabits per second.

■ *Applications*

2G products offer only voice and Short Message Service (SMS).

2.5G products add e-mail and other data service features.

3G products offer multimedia services and interactive games.

■ *Products*

2G phones are mobile phones (analog only) with voice service.

2.5G phones offer voice and data features and could fall into the "smart phone" category with personal digital assistant (PDA) functionality.

3G phones add high-speed data transmission with Internet access, multimedia, and videoconferencing features.

The promise of 3G is huge. According to Nokia's Web site, "3G is videoconferencing in a taxi. 3G is watching clips from your favorite soap in the train. 3G is sending images straight from the field to headquarters for analysis. 3G is sharing your Moroccan vacation with your friend—from Morocco."

User applications for 3G include:

- Local-area network access, enabling users to wirelessly transfer data, share resources (such as printers), and access e-mail and corporate information in a campus environment

- Internet applications, including Web browsing, e-mail, video telephone, news reports, and networked games

- Video conferencing

- Transmission of short messages and personal information in the form of wireless post cards and business cards—for example, at conferences or trade shows

As mobile phones begin taking on more 3G-design concepts, their performance will step up in several important categories. These include:

- Support for high-speed data services

- Global standards promoting functional commonality

- Enhanced flexibility for future design evolution

- Improved spectrum efficiency

- Wider range of features and services

An open-systems architecture would permit the easy introduction and transition to new advances in technology.

12.2 When will 3G-level devices be available?

3G-level wireless devices are not likely to begin to appear on the market until sometime in 2002, probably even later in the United States. Much of the delay is attributed to the lack of availability of equipment—both handsets and network infrastructure—and to problems with software that controls the "handoff" of calls from cell to cell. Also, it is unlikely that 3G will be rolled out to new subscribers everywhere at the same time, which means that some people will continue to use 2G or 2.5G. Some may even use "hybrid" wireless models, which embody the best features of 2.5G and some elements of 3G, as equipment manufacturers and network operators work to upgrade their products and services. In addition, surveys reveal that much work needs to be done to educate consumers on the availability and "value" of 3G services.

■ 3G won't take off in the United States until at least 2003.

Tell Me More

Most of today's most advanced wireless models, including mobile phones offering data services with more features and functions, so-called smart phones, are at the 2.5G level of development. These are expected to dominate the market through at least 2003 in the United States. In 2002, only Japan's wireless infrastructure is scheduled to take on some of the structure and features of 3G technologies. But even Japan will not adopt 3G as rapidly as initially expected, mainly because of technical problems. Europe, which is off to a rough start with 3G, will follow Japan in deploying 3G systems.

Finland telecom operator Sonera liquidated its 3G joint venture with Enitel in Norway and returned its 3G telecom license to the Norwegian government when it failed to win a 3G license from Sweden. Sonera said its decision to exit its deal in Norway was based on winning 3G licenses in Finland, Norway, and Sweden.

The United States, mainly for economic reasons and an ongoing regulatory debate over the need for additional spectrum to support 3G services, will delay the full rollout of 3G until 2003, or later.

12.3 What is convergence?

Historically, *convergence* has meant the integration of computers and communications. In simpler terms, it usually refers to combining the functions of these two products into a single product. This could include hardware or software.

An easy example is a "smart phone" that functions as both a cellular phone (communications) and as a personal digital assistant (a computer). In some industry circles, convergence has also come to mean multimedia, as in the integration of voice, data, audio, and video into a single device or service. More recently, some companies and analysts are using "convergence" to describe the merging of wireless communications with the Internet, leading eventually to remotely (wirelessly)-controlled Internet-enabled appliances.

- For most manufacturers, convergence means differentiating their product from the competition by adding new features.

- Convergence raises questions about creating new business models for how people will use this technology.

Tell Me More

As the technology allows, mobile device manufacturers will continue to differentiate and add value to their products by adding new features. In addition to integrating a cellphone and PDA into the same handheld device, future devices might also include MP3 players and Global Positioning System (GPS) navigational aids as standard equipment.

Is this Swiss Army knife approach to developing new mobile devices a good or a bad thing? Consumer surveys have been mixed: some people prefer a dedicated mobile device, such as a cellphone, just for voice communications. Others want a more highly featured device, such as a "smart phone," that functions as a cellphone and a PDA. A good example is the Kyocera Smartphone. It doubles as a phone and PDA and features a mobile Internet browser that downloads full-text versions of Web pages in the HTML language used on computers. If early reviews and its success in the marketplace are any indication, the Kyocera model will lead to a growing variety of this class of device from different manufacturers and will include several integrated features and functions, such as GPS for navigation capability, a built-in digital camera, MP3 for music, Bluetooth for short-range networking, and wireless e-mail and Internet access.

Convergence is likely to affect much more than product design and development and marketing methods. Lucent Technologies has provided $10 million in funding for a research program called the Mobility Innovation Initiative, which is aimed at exploring the effects of mobility on businesses and consumers. The program will operate through grants to the School of Management at Boston University, London Business School, and France's INSEAD Business School. Lucent hopes that this research will result in the development of new business models to take advantage of the opportunities created by 3G wireless networks. Results of the program are expected to influence Lucent's in-house R&D by Bell Labs and, longer term, its business models.

An in-depth study in early 2000 by Accenture, a management consulting firm, offers some mixed signals on convergence. Researchers found that only about 5 percent of U.S. cellphone owners use their phones for e-mail, and even fewer use them for accessing the Web. But it also showed that more than a quarter of PDA owners in the United States use them for e-mail. Far fewer PDA users, 16 percent, use them for checking news, stocks, or sports scores.

At the same time, Accenture says that wireless and consumer electronics companies are finding that much of their success depends on offering a variety of highly differentiated products and services. The market for digital mobile devices is expected to double its growth between 2000 and 2001, but the consulting firm says this will only occur if companies can accurately predict what business professionals and consumers want and need and provide these products in a timely fashion.

To help better understand mobile convergence and fuel its growth worldwide, the U.S.-based Personal Communications Industry Association has formed the PCUA Global Initiative. Its members come from virtually every industry involved in mobile communications, including content providers, wireless carriers, network computing vendors, payment solution companies, software developers, device and semiconductor manufacturers, application service providers, and Internet service providers. Through the association, member companies will have access to customized, global consumer, marketplace data, and synthesized global regulatory and technical data.

12.4 What is involved in switching from 2G to 3G mobile service?

The migration from 2G analog cellular service—the level of cellular phones most people are using today—to 2.5G, which embodies mostly phones with both analog and digital functionality, and then to the more advanced 3G systems and services is going to be a long one, especially in the United States.

- Interoperability of networks and terminals made by different manufacturers will be required for 3G services to function.

- Costs for obtaining the needed spectrum allocation to offer 3G are proving to be very high.

- Manufacturers are not producing 3G-ready equipment as fast as some wireless carriers would like.

Tell Me More

The path to 3G has not been a smooth one, with a running debate over which digital transmission standard to support for 3G service. The issue is as much about cost as it is about technology. Operators of CDMA-based digital networks have a single path to 3G. The technologies available to CDMA operators are backward compatible, enabling them to communicate in any area served by 3G-level CDMA mobile devices. GSM and TDMA operators have multiple choices in how they can implement 3G. Also, there are multiple issues involved. For example, Wideband CDMA (WCDMA), the 3G solution for GSM and TDMA, is incompatible with GPRS and EDGE, which are based on the GSM standard. And GPRS and EDGE both will require new handsets.

Agreeing on a single technical standard for 3G has been the most contentious issue among equipment manufacturers and network operators. In an alphabet soup of high-tech acronyms that could easily challenge the U.S. military, the spectrum, standards, networks, terminal types, and services that comprise the 2.5G and 3G wireless categories include:

■ *Air interfaces.* GPRS, HSCSD, EDGE, IS-95B, 1xRTT, HDR, 1xEvolution, (1xEV), 1XTREME, W-CDMA (IMT DS), cdma2000 (IMT MC), UTRA TDD (IMT TC), DECT, UWC-136, and OFDM.

■ *Spectrum bands.* 746–806 MHz, 824–894 MHz, 1850–1990 MHz, 2500–2690 MHz, 1710–1755 MHz, 1755–1850 MHz, 2110–2150 MHz, and 2160–2165 MHz.

■ *Terminal browser, language, and operating system choices.* WAP/WML, STK, Palm, EPOC, MS, Microware, GEOS, HDML, i-mode, cHTML, BREW, and proprietary formats.

■ *Network architectures.* GSM MAP, IS-41, and IP cores.

■ *Terminal types.* Smartphones, Web-enabled phones, PDA/handhelds, notebook computers, pagers, mobile phones, and Internet appliances.

■ *Middleware.* Oracle, Aether, AvantGo, JP Systems, Mobilware, Infospace, and MobilQ.

There are a number of rival standards helping get 3G functionality off the ground. Standards associations and regulators will need to work together to bring the standards being developed by different countries together in one unified technical standard if 3G is ever to really take off. The International Mobile Telecommunications-2000 (IMT-2000) will provide the framework for 3G networks, including Europe's UMTS and W-CDMA, which is favored by Japan's standards body. These standards will be harmonized in the Third Generation Partnership Project (3GPP), the global body currently dedicated to the development of 3G specifications.

Each standard is supported by one or more standards development organizations, and each of these groups has had various levels of success in promoting its standard for 3G services.

GSM vs. TDMA One of the important developments is that full interoperability between GSM and TDMA (GSM is a derivative technology of

TDMA) is on track for the end of 2001, although it will take time for equipment manufacturers and network operators to integrate the technology into their products and services. Also, questions remain about how quickly consumers and even professional users of mobile services will adopt 3G; in other words, more than just technical and economic issues are in play here—marketing decisions will have to be made concerning the timing of the rollout of 3G products and services. This will likely vary around the world.

At last count, there were more than 393 million GSM subscribers in the world, compared to 61 million TDMA subscribers. Of those 61 million TDMA subscribers worldwide at the end of 2000, about half were in North America. GSM service is available in the 48 contiguous U.S. states and six Canadian provinces, and more than 10 million subscribers now use GSM technology in North America, according to GSM North America. Several North American wireless operators, such as AT&T Wireless, Rogers Wireless in Canada, and Telcel in Mexico, plan to add GSM service.

Testimony submitted to the Federal Communications Commission by the CDMA Development Group points out that global roaming within the U.S. cellular and PCS frequency bands, which were included in the bands identified by the ITU for IMT-2000, will be difficult to achieve because the use of these particular bands differs across various regions. Many countries in the Americas (namely Argentina, Canada, Chile, Mexico, and Peru) will allow cellular and PCS operations in the 800 MHz and 1850–1990 MHz bands to upgrade their systems to 3G in those bands as market needs arise.

In addition, many countries in the Americas are considering using the 1710–1850 MHz band for additional frequencies for IMT-2000, although some countries are considering pairing portions of that band with the 2110–2200 MHz band. Although this would enable a "global" downlink in the 2110–2200 MHz band, the problem, as the CDG sees it, is that the integrity of the European DCS-1800 band, and any in-band pairing associated with that band, would be lost. In fact, much of the decision of whether pairing that follows the European DCS-1800 band plan is chosen for the United States depends on the availability of the U.S. Government's parts of the 1755–1850 MHz band.

Against that background, the CDG believes that to facilitate global roaming and gain economies of scale, spectrum decisions in the United States should be aligned as much as possible with national decisions resulting from the World Radio Communications Conference–2000.

GSM vs. CDMA Meanwhile, the GSM Roaming Forum, in addition to making GSM and TDMA interoperable, is pursuing a similar effort with CDMA. After six years of commercial deployment, CDMA has 71 million subscribers. CDMA technologies are licensed to more than 75 communications equipment manufacturers worldwide.

Finally, there is the very difficult issue of migrating from IPv4 to IPv6.

12.5 Where does IPv6 fit into 3G?

IPv6, or Internet Protocol version 6, is the standard proposed by the Internet Engineering Task Force to address problems from the previous Internet Protocol, IPv4, introduced in 1978. The biggest issue is that IPv4 is running out of numbers, or addresses, and it cannot handle the growing number of wireless devices that will connect to the Internet in the next few years. Meanwhile, the Third Generation Partnership Project (3GPP), the standards forum for 3G, has mandated IPv6, which is expected to help speed the integration of the Internet and 3G services.

- Developing an all-Internet Protocol is next on the agenda for providing new IP-based services for new terminals.

- Some organizations, anticipating a near-term shortage of Internet addresses, are adopting an interim technology.

Tell Me More

The first implementation of an Internet Protocol based on IPv6 is expected in 2002. Several wireless equipment manufacturers and network operators believe the adoption of IPv6 is critical to the success of 3G.

Some organizations who are anticipating a near-term shortage of Internet addresses have begun to use what is called network-address-translation (NAT) technology, in which companies can create large numbers of private, unregistered Internet addresses for internal use. These addresses can be linked to the Internet through public, registered addresses. However, IPv6 proponents believe that NAT is vulnerable to network security and other technical problems.

12.6 Will 3G require the allocation of new radio frequency spectrum?

The assumption has always been that 3G would require additional radio spectrum to meet the demands of the system.

- Manufacturers have been developing solutions that could bypass the need for additional spectrum for 3G systems, but with mixed success.

- The FCC was scheduled to conduct a spectrum auction in September 2002; however, wireless carriers have requested that the auction be delayed.

- The wireless industry has attempted to get the Pentagon to give up some of its assigned spectrum to commercial applications.

- A memo by former President Clinton articulates the need to accommodate additional spectrum to meet the country's future mobile communications service requirements.

Tell Me More

It has been generally assumed that 3G will require the allocation of more of the radio spectrum. This is true, not only in the United States, but also in Europe and eventually in other regions of the world. However, efforts by mobile wireless interests in the United States to obtain new spectrum for 3G services have been challenged by commercial broadcasters and other dedicated wireless service users—such as fixed wireless local area network (WLAN), mobile satellite operators, public safety agencies, and government agencies (including the Pentagon)—who are reluctant to give up any of the spectrum currently assigned to them.

Anticipating that this could slow the deployment of 3G globally, the industry's leading infrastructure manufacturers have been developing solutions that could bypass the need for additional spectrum for 3G systems, but with mixed success.

In March 2001, the FCC began the process of reallocating television channels 52–59 (in the 698–746 MHz spectrum band) for new commercial wireless (including 3G) and broadcast services.

In part, the FCC is having a hard time finding spectrum to allocate to 3G because of the current demands of the television broadcasting industry. The U.S. Congress agreed to allow broadcasters to retain their analog channels until they complete their transition to digital TV. During this transition period broadcasters may continue to operate their existing analog systems while using a second channel to transmit their DTV signals. So they are essentially using two channels each and are therefore reluctant to give up spectrum for mobile 3G services. Although all broadcasters must offer a digital signal by 2002, they don't have to give up their analog spectrum until the digital transition is completed, which is scheduled to take place by the end in 2006. So there is no reason to think that they will be any more willing to give up spectrum before then.

At the same time, the FCC proposed the licensing of and competitive bidding for wireless and other licenses in this 48 MHz of spectrum, which the wireless industry viewed as a threat to its ability to obtain additional spectrum for new services. Indeed, the FCC said that it was reclaiming the spectrum for new commercial services as part of its transition of TV broadcasting from analog to digital TV (DTV) transmission systems. To further complicate matters, the Telecommunications Act requires the FCC to assign spectrum by auctions in the 700 MHz band (698–806 MHz) that television broadcasters were able to reclaim as part of their transition from analog to digital TV transmission systems. The FCC is scheduled to conduct its auction in September 2002, although wireless carriers, mostly for economic reasons related to the high cost of obtaining new licenses and upgrading their networks for next-generation services, have requested that the auction be delayed.

The complications don't end there. The FCC is statutorily required to extend the date that a broadcaster can operate its analog station, on a market-by-market basis, if one or more of the four largest network stations or affiliates are not broadcasting in digital technology, if digital-to-analog converter technology is not generally available, or if 15 percent or more of television households in the market are not receiving a digital signal. At the end of the transition to digital TV, analog service will cease, and the remaining broadcast operations above Channel 51 are to be relocated. Analog will disappear, to be replaced by an all-digital TV system.

The wireless industry, needless to say, is not happy with all the delays in finding spectrum to allocate to its services. The industry is particularly concerned about "the 15 percent rule" that allows broadcasters to retain their analog channels if 15 percent of houses in the market don't have digital TV. According to the wireless industry, the market-by-market provision means that one region may receive close to 100 percent digital TV coverage, while another receives only 30 percent market penetration. In the view of wireless carriers, the broadcasters are simply another impediment to their acquiring additional spectrum for new services, particularly 3G.

The wireless industry, led by the Personal Communications Industry Association (PCIA) has also attempted to persuade the U.S. Department of Defense to give up some of its vast spectrum resources for commercial wireless applications. However, the DOD has indicated that it has no plans to give up any of its 1755–1850 MHz band service.

The Clinton Memorandum. In yet another complication, prior to leaving office on October 13, 2000, President Clinton issued a memorandum articulating the need to select radio spectrum that would satisfy the United States' future needs for mobile voice, high-speed data, and Internet-accessible wireless capability.

The Clinton memorandum established "guiding principles" for executive agencies to use in selecting spectrum that could be made available for 3G wireless systems. The memo strongly encouraged independent federal agencies to follow the same principles in any actions they take related to the development of 3G systems.

Noting the joint spectrum management responsibilities of the Executive Branch and the FCC, the memorandum directed the Secretary of Commerce to work with the FCC in several areas. The National Telecommunications and Information Administration (NTIA), an agency of the U.S.

Commerce Department, manages spectrum use by U.S. government agencies and serves as the telecommunications policy advisor to the President.

One of these areas of cooperation calls for selecting spectrum for 3G wireless systems. Another suggests issuing an interim report on the current spectrum uses and potential for reallocation or sharing of the frequency bands identified at the 2000 World Radiocommunications Conference that could be used for 3G systems.

However, with a new Administration and new leadership at the FCC, the Clinton memo is likely to lie dormant.

The FCC, DOD, and NTIA Response. The follow-up to the Clinton proposals came on March 30, 2001, when three federal government agencies—the NTIA, the FCC, and the Department of Defense (DOD)—released studies strongly suggesting that the Clinton Administration's proposals for 3G services probably won't work.

The NTIA's report was a technical analysis of the potential for 3G systems operating without causing interference with a radio frequency band now used exclusively for military radio communications by the DOD and other federal government agencies. Limited sharing of government-controlled radio frequency bands between commercial and government users and band segmentation to accommodate high-speed mobile Internet service in the United States, the NTIA report added, may be possible under certain conditions that will be explored further.

To the U.S. telecom industry, all the reports cast further doubt that spectrum will be made available in time for the FCC to conduct auctions for spectrum designated for 3G services in the United States in September of 2002 as planned.

The FCC, in response to the Clinton memorandum, said that it will consider five frequency bands for 3G services:

1710–1755 MHz

1755–1780 MHz

2100–2150 MHz

2160–2165 MHz

2500–2690 MHz

However, as already indicated, the memorandum called for auctioning licenses for 3G services by September, 2002, leaving little time to identify 3G spectrum and giving incumbent users little time to vacate those frequency bands and move into new ones.

Another issue, and one that is being contested within the wireless industry, is how much spectrum will actually be needed for 3G. With industry projections of more than 600 million 3G subscribers worldwide by 2010, the Cellular Telecommunications and Internet Association (CTIA) suggests that wireless providers will need "a substantial amount of additional spectrum." The mobile sector of the wireless industry may have to go through some lengthy negotiations to obtain this additional spectrum.

12.7 What will Fourth-Generation mobile technology be like?

Even though 3G mobile systems are a long way from being widely deployed, several wireless systems manufacturers and their technical forums are already thinking seriously about what form Fourth Generation (4G) mobile services will take.

- The first goal of 4G would be to boost the data rate over 3G service to at least 10 megabits per second.

- 4G proponents hope to integrate virtually all commercial wireless networks into one seamless compatible system.

- Several major telecom companies have formed an organization to develop 4G technologies.

- There will clearly be major difficulties finding enough spectrum for such an ambitious system.

Tell Me More

One of the goals of 4G mobile services is to significantly boost the data rate, at least to 10 megabits per second and possibly as high as 100 mbps. It is most likely that 4G would also embody software-defined radio (SDR) techniques to quickly and seamlessly make over-the-air software fixes and deliver new applications to cellular phones and other wireless devices.

Fourth Generation will also integrate virtually all commercial wireless networks, including cellular, PCS, Bluetooth, wireless local area networks, mobile satellite communications, and even radio and TV broadcasts, into a single mobile system.

Still another idea for 4G is to integrate its wireless voice mail with home, office, and other mobile services, allowing the user to have one password for all of these environments.

Several major telecom companies, including Alcatel, Ericsson, Nokia, and Siemens, have formed the Wireless World Research Forum to develop 4G technologies. Also, Hewlett-Packard and Japan's leading wireless carrier, NTT DoCoMo, have announced a joint research program to develop multimedia over 4G systems, including advanced mobile printing, scanning, and copying services. The companies say they will "explore new mobile concepts" in both the real and cyber worlds. The HP/NTT plan is to create an architecture, which they call MOTO-Media, to deliver streaming media to mobile devices that would make "optimal use of network resources." The two companies expect to wrap up their 4G research program by 2003.

Meanwhile, 4G, referred to by some industry analysts as the "next next generation," raises many questions. Will there be a 3.5G before a 4G, and where will the spectrum come from to accommodate 4G mobile communications requirement? Of course, no one knows, but if history holds true to form there is time to figure it out. Most "generations" last about ten years. That gives 4G researchers until about 2010 to come up with new, very highly featured and high-speed products and services.

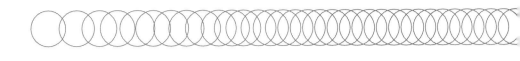

Glossary of Terms, Acronyms, and Abbreviations

Access point   A centrally located transceiver (transmitter/receiver) that provides wireless terminals, such as cellular phones and wireless-enabled laptop computers, access to a local or regional wireless network. Starbucks, for example, plans to install access points, which look like smoke detectors and are usually mounted on a wall, in their coffee houses for sending and receiving data to and from their customers' portable wireless devices.

Air interface   The transmission system of a wireless network. Common wireless air interfaces include AMPS, CDMA, TDMA, and GSM.

Airtime   The time that a wireless phone is connected and in use for talking or transmitting and receiving data.

Allocation   The assignment of a band of frequencies for a specific radio service or services. The Federal Communications Commission (FCC) is responsible for frequency allocations in the United States. However, the National Telecommunications and Information

Administration (NTIA), an agency of the U.S. Department of Commerce, oversees frequency assignments for federal agencies, and advises the President on national telecommunications policy.

Alphanumeric   A display, message, or readout that contains both letters and numbers. Used with text paging or messaging.

American National Standards Institute (ANSI)   A nonprofit organization that coordinates the development of U.S. voluntary national technical standards. ANSI is the U.S. representative to non-treaty international standards-setting bodies, including the International Organization for Standardization (ISO).

AMPS (Advanced Mobile Phone Service)   Introduced in the United States in 1983, AMPS is the first generation cellular phone system. It is the U.S. technical standard for analog cellular phones. It also is used in Latin America, the Asia/Pacific, Russia, and other areas of the world.

Analog   The original method of transmitting voice signals over cellular and cordless phones. AM (amplitude modulation) and FM (frequency modulation) are the most common methods of analog modulation of a radio signal. Most U.S. cellular systems continue to carry analog phone conversations, even though virtually all U.S. systems have switched or are switching to digital networks.

Application Service Provider (ASP)   ASPs provide a variety of telecommunications outsourcing services to corporations, ranging from e-mail and other messaging to document and image management, software application development, sales force automation software, and customer relationship management software. In some cases, ASPs also manage corporations' accounting, payroll, and human resources activities.

Authentication   The process of verifying the identity of the telecom device user at the other end of a communications or computer link. Authentication is accomplished by using a link key stored in the device memory or by a user personal identify number (PIN). Authentication is a fundamental part of many cryptography systems.

B2B   Business-to-business

B2C   Business-to-consumer

B2G   Business-to-government

Bandwidth   The measure of the carrying capacity, or size of a communications channel. The bandwidth of a radio signal is determined by the amount of information in the signal that is being transmitted.

Base station   The central radio transmitter/receiver that maintains communications with mobile radios within a given range (typically, a cell site).

Big LEO   Low-earth orbit (approximately 420 nautical miles) satellite system that offers voice and data services. The main differences between Big LEOs (low-earth orbit) satellites and Little LEOs is that Big LEOs provide both voice and data services and operate above 1 gigahertz (GHz), and Little LEOs provide only data services and operate below 1 GHz.

Bit   A single digital number in binary numbering; in other words, either a 1 or a 0.

Bits per second (bps)   A measure of data transmission speed; the number of binary digits that can be sent through a channel per second.

Bluetooth   A low-power, short-range (10 meters, although this may be extended to 100 meters) wireless technology designed for local area voice and data communications. Promoted initially by Ericsson, Nokia, IBM, Intel, and Toshiba, Bluetooth is being developed as an open (nonproprietary) standard wireless communications link between devices such as smart phones, personal digital assistants (PDAs), laptop and notebook computers, personal computers, and other wireless devices. A key characteristic of Bluetooth is that it enables these devices to detect and communicate with each other unconsciously or without user intervention once they are in range of each other. Despite well-publicized delays, the rollout of Bluetooth products is expected to begin in earnest by the end of 2001.

The Bluetooth Special Interest Group (SIG) now has more than 2,000 company members.

Broadband   A communications channel with a bandwidth greater than 674 kilobits per second (kbps) that can provide high-speed data communications via standard telephone circuits.

Browser   A software program that enables users to view and interact with virtually any Internet resource that is available on the World Wide Web (WWW).

Carrier   A local or regional communications service provider.

CDMA (code division multiple access)   CDMA is an advanced digital technology that converts audio signals into a stream of digital information (made up of 1s and 0s). The digital transmission operates over a wideband channel consisting of several radio frequencies. CDMA differs from other popular digital cellular platforms in that it uses several frequencies instead of just one. CDMA signals are encoded and spread across a wide bandwidth, then reconstituted at the receiving end. One of the features of CDMA is that it has at least ten times the transmission capacity of analog systems.

cdma2000   Cdma2000 is a Third Generation (3G) technical standard for the delivery of high bandwidth data and high capacity voice services. It will enable data throughput of 2 mbps and higher. Cdma2000 also allows simultaneous access to several voice, video, and data services. It is fully compliant with International Mobile Telecommunications-2000 (IMT-2000) derived from International Telecommunications Union (ITU) requirements for 3G. The first phase of 3G for cdma2000 networks is designated 1X; 1XEV is the evolutionary phase for 3G for cdma2000 networks. 1XEV is divided into two phases—1XEV-DO (data only), and 1XEV-DC (data and voice).

Cell   The geographic area served by a single low-power transmitter/receiver. A cellular system's service area is divided into multiple, overlapping cells. Cellular calls are "handed off" during a conversation when a cellphone user moves from one cell to another.

Cellular digital packet data (CDPD)   A digital packet data protocol designed to efficiently carry data on existing analog (AMPS) or
digital time division multiple access (TDMA) cellular radio systems.
Introduced in 1992, and now available in most geographic areas of
the United States, CDPD uses the idle time in the analog cellular
system to transmit data in "packets" at rates up to 19.2 kilobits per
second.

Certificate   A file, digitally signed by a Certification Authority. There
are many different types of certificates.

Certification Authority (CA)   The trusted entity that signs and
issues public key (secure) certificates and takes liability associated
with the validity of the holder's identity.

Channel   A path, or radio frequency, over which a communications
signal is transmitted.

Chip   An integrated electronic circuit (IC) in which millions of active
or passive elements can be fabricated and connected on a continuous substrate, as opposed to a discrete electronic component, such
as a resistor, capacitor, or diode.

Circuit-switched   A switched circuit that is maintained only while
the transmitter and receiver are communicating, as opposed to a
dedicated circuit which is held open whether data is being sent or
not. Circuit-switching is used in standard telephone service. However, as wireless systems advance and new mobile applications
emerge, circuit-switching is losing ground to packet-switching, a
technology used for communications over the Internet.

Commercial Mobile Radio Service   The regulatory classification
used by the Federal Communications Commission (FCC) to govern
all commercial wireless service providers, including cellular, Personal
Communications Service (PCS), and Enhanced Specialized Mobile
Radio (ESMR).

Cordless   A term generally applied to radio technology in which a
wireless handset is used within a restricted distance from its base

station. Most currently available cordless phones operate at 900 MHz.

Cryptography   The process of ensuring that messages are secure. In public telecom networks, voice and data messages can be mathematically encrypted (scrambled) in a way that makes them unreadable except to someone who has access to the mathematical key that can decrypt (unscramble) it. Cryptographic systems are based on the concepts of authentication, integrity, confidentiality, and non-repudiation.

CT-2   Cordless telephone–second generation (CT-2) is a digital cordless telephone standard. It was originally developed for use with the short-range Telepoint system in the United Kingdom. CT-2 phone users can initiate calls, but cannot receive them.

CTIA (Cellular Telecommunications and Internet Association) Formerly the Cellular Telecommunications Industry Association, the CTIA is a U.S.-based international trade association that represents all elements of mobile communications—cellular, personal communications services (PCS), Enhanced Specialized Mobile Radio (ESMR), and mobile satellite services.

Database   A central computerized repository for digital information that can be updated and extracted from virtually anywhere by remote access.

Data connectivity   The ability of a device to transmit and receive data. Most of the newer wireless phones offer data connectivity in that they can send faxes, access the Internet, and send and check e-mail.

Data Encryption Standard (DES)   The most widely used secret key encryption algorithm (a 56-bit key). One version of DES, called triple DES (or 3DES), is used in bank cards.

Data interface   A device that connects a computer to a cellular phone for data transmission. It works similarly to a modem.

DCS (Digital Cellular System) 1800   *See* GSM 1800

DECT (Digital European Cordless Telecommunications)　A digital cordless telecom system intended initially for wireless private branch exchange (PBX) applications. However, this service may be used in the consumer market. DECT supports both voice and data communications

Digital　A method of transmitting voice or data using the computer's binary code of 0s and 1s. For wireless communications purposes, digital transmissions offer a clearer signal and more capacity than analog technology. Cellular systems providing digital transmission are currently in operation throughout most developed countries of the world and will eventually become available in less developed areas. Code division multiple access (CDMA), time division multiple access (TDMA), the Global System for Mobile Communications (GSM), and Japan's Personal Handyphone System (PHS) are digital systems.

Digital imaging　In mobile device terms, digital imaging usually means a digital camera. In fact, some personal digital assistants (PDAs) are now available with digital cameras either built into them or as clip-on attachments. A survey by the Consumer Electronics Association indicates that 80 percent of digital camera owners have e-mailed a photo taken with a digital camera.

Digital modulation　A method of encoding information for transmission that offers greater capacity, better quality, and permits more services than analog systems.

Digital signatures　Digital signatures are used to ensure the authenticity and integrity of documents and electronic transactions transmitted over wired or wireless networks. They are based on public key encryption which is used to scramble electronically transmitted information so that only the designated recipient can read it. Digital signatures are now protected by the Electronic Signatures in Global and National Commerce Act, which became law in October 2000. The act makes it legal to conduct consumer-to-business (apply for a loan or an insurance policy) or business-to-business (transmit a signed order or contract) transactions.

Displays   Cellular phones, personal digital assistants (PDAs), and other wireless devices use a variety of display technologies, most of which are similar to those used in handheld calculators and other portable electronic devices. The most popular of these are LCDs (liquid crystal displays) and LED (light emitting diode) displays. A more recently development is "virtual displays," which will enable graphics (charts, tables, and blueprints) and still pictures to be transmitted wirelessly and viewed through a camcorder-like eyepiece.

Downlink   The radio signal path from a satellite to an earth station. (The uplink, of course, is the path from the earth station to the satellite.)

Dual-mode phone   A phone that operates on both analog and digital networks.

E-911   Enhanced-911 service features automatic number identification and automatic location information for 911 operators. E-911 enables cellular phone users to make emergency calls without knowing their precise location, which can usually be determined by the satellite-based Global Positioning System (GPS), or by triangulating signal strength from cellular base stations closest to the caller.

Earth station   An assembly of radio equipment, antennae, and satellite communication and control systems that provide access from terrestrial radio links to a satellite.

E-commerce (electronic commerce)   E-commerce refers to conducting business online via the Web. Related terms that are commonly used in the same context are "e-business" and "e-tailing" for online retailing. In the mobile environment, the term most commonly used is mobile commerce, or m-commerce.

EDGE (enhanced data rates for GSM evolution)   EDGE is a higher speed version (384 kilobits per second) of the current Global System for Mobile Communications (GSM) digital wireless service. EDGE will operate with both General Packet Radio Service (GPRS) and circuit-switched data networks.

E-mail (electronic mail)   Messages, usually text, sent from one person to another over a local-area network (LAN) or over the Internet.

Encryption   The process of "scrambling" a message to prevent it from being read by unauthorized parties.

EPOC   An operating system that is an open platform for mobile multimedia terminals. EPOC is being developed by Symbian, a joint venture of Psion, Nokia, Ericsson, Motorola, and Matsushita Electric (Panasonic).

E-purse   *See E-wallet.*

European Telecommunications Standards Institute (ETSI)   Based in France, ETSI is one of the European organizations responsible for establishing common, industrywide technical standards for telecommunications services in Europe. It was the standards body responsible for the development and approval of the Global System for Mobile Communications (GSM) throughout Europe.

E-wallet   A small, portable device that contains electronic money, typically stored in a bank account or on a smart card.

Extensible markup language (XML)   XML is one of the building blocks of websites that tells browsers how data should be displayed on a screen. It also describes the content and structure of the information. It is extensible because it enables developers to customize the language for their specific data interchange needs. XML is expected to become the standard for automating data exchange between business systems.

Federal Communications Commission (FCC)   The FCC is the government agency primarily responsible for regulating telecommunications in the United States, including the allocation of radio spectrum for mobile communications technologies.

Firewall   Located on a network, a firewall is a set of related programs that protects the resources of a private network. Essentially, it prevents outsiders from other networks from accessing private data resources and controls what outside resources the network's own users can access. It resides between an organization's internal network and the Internet. It is designed to protect unauthorized access to a company's network, mainly by hackers using the Internet.

FLEX   A Motorola-developed global de facto messaging protocol for high-speed, one-way alphanumeric paging. FLEX gives service providers more capacity and faster transmission times than earlier generation paging products. Extensions of FLEX include InFLEX, which enables transmission and storage of voice messages, and ReFLEX, a two-way alphanumeric paging protocol.

Frequency   A measure of energy, in one or more waves per second, in an electrical or lightwave information signal. A signal's frequency is stated in Hertz (Hz), or cycles per second.

Frequency hopping   A spread spectrum technique in which the signal between the base radio station and the subscriber unit (cellular phone or other type of mobile/portable communications device) hops from frequency to frequency simultaneously. This technique was developed during World War II to prevent jamming of radio signals and to ensure secure radio communications. A version of frequency hopping is now used in code division multiple access (CDMA) digital cellular transmissions.

Function keys   The non-numeric keys on a mobile phone used to access and navigate menu features as well as to perform memory functions.

GAIT (GSM/ANSI-136 Interoperability Team)   A group dedicated to bring interoperability to GSM and TDMA cellular systems. GAIT has been active since 1999, working mainly with the GSM Association and the U.S.-based TDMA organization, the Universal Wireless Communications Association.

Gateway   Essentially, an earth (or ground) station that links a satellite or satellites with the terrestrial public telephone network. Gateways can also be part of a local area network (LAN) that enables it to interface with different networks.

General Packet Radio Service (GPRS)   GPRS is an enhancement to existing GSM and TDMA networks that introduces packet-linked technology at high speed (115 kilobits per second). A key feature of GPRS is that it is "always on," meaning that users are always connected and can choose to be permanently logged on to e-mail, Internet access, and other services. When EDGE is added to GPRS, the data rate will increase to up to 384 kbps.

Geostationary satellite   A satellite whose speed is synchronized with the earth's rotation so that the satellite is always in the same location over the earth. Most geostationary communications satellites orbit the earth at an altitude of approximately 22,300 miles.

GHz (Gigahertz)   A frequency equal to one billion Hertz, or cycles per second.

GLONASS   GLONASS is Russia's satellite-based global navigation system. Like the U.S. GPS satellite navigation network, it uses twenty-four satellites, although they often are not in operation at the same time.

GPS (Global Positioning System)   A network of twenty-four navigational satellites developed and operated by the U.S. Department of Defense. The GPS provides precise location determination anywhere in the world via special receivers, which can indicate the location of a aircraft, ship, or people with an accuracy of within one hundred meters. Increasingly, GPS is being used for commercial purposes (such as surveying), recreational activities (boating and hiking), and personal applications (in-vehicle navigation). It is also being adopted for Enhanced-911 services in the United States.

GSM (Global System for Mobile Communications)   Originally called the Groupe Speciale Mobile, GSM is the pan-European digital cellular standard. Several service providers in the United States also use GSM, but at a different frequency from that used in Europe.

GSM 900   GSM 900 is the world's most widely used digital mobile network. It operates in more than one hundred countries around the world, particularly in Europe and Asia Pacific.

GSM 1800   Also known as DCS 1800 or PCN, GSM 1800 is a digital network that operates in the 1800 MHz frequency band. It is used in Europe, Asia-Pacific, and Australia.

GSM 1900   Also, known as PCS 1900, GSM 1900 is a digital network working on a frequency of 1900 MHz. It is used in the United States and Canada, and is expected to become operational in parts of Latin America and Africa.

GSM Global Roaming Forum   Launched in June 2000 by the GSM Association, the GSM Global Roaming Forum is comprised of companies with roaming products and services from GSM, iDEN, CDMA, TETRA, and TDMA technologies. The mission of the forum is to develop technical requirements for terminals, networking, and smart cards, as well as commercial standards for services, billing, financial settlements, and fraud management.

GUI (graphical user interface)   A graphics-based interface uses icons, menus and a mouse to manage and control interaction with the system. Functionally, it substitutes graphics for characters.

Handoff   Cellular systems are designed so that a phone call can continue while driving or walking from one area of cellular transmission coverage, or "cell," to another cell. The mobile radio remains on a specific channel until the strength of the signal begins to weaken, at which point it automatically switches to another channel in the next, adjacent cell. The seamless transfer of the call from cell to cell is called a handoff.

Hands-free operation   Allows the mobile phone user to conduct a conversation without holding the cellular phone, usually because the phone is in a special cradle and attached to an earphone.

HDML (Handheld Device Markup Language)   A modification of standard HTML, HDML is a text-based markup language that uses

HyperText Transfer Protocol (HTTP) and is compatible with Web servers. It was developed by Unwired Planet for use on small screens of mobile phones, PDAs, and pagers.

Hertz (Hz)   The unit of measuring frequency signals. One Hertz is equal to one cycle per second.

HomeRF   A standard that provides data services, Internet connectivity, entertainment, and wireless telecom connections, principally in the small office and home environment. It also serves file transfer and resource sharing (such as printers) without external wiring. HomeRF was initially conceived for use in small office/home office (SOHO) applications with multiple, networked PCs. The technology is represented by the HomeRF Working Group.

HTML (HyperText Markup Language)   HTML is the method by which information is presented through Web sites and viewed in a standard format no matter what type of computer is being used.

HyperText Transfer Protocol (HTTP)   The protocol used by the Web server and the client browser to communicate and move documents around the Internet.

iDEN (Integrated Digital Enhanced Network)   A digital wireless technology developed by Motorola to enable multiple services to be delivered from a single, integrated wireless communications system. It is the backbone of the all-digital Nextel Communications system.

IEEE (Institute of Electrical and Electronics Engineers)   The IEEE is the largest technical society in the world with more than 320,000 members, mostly electronics engineers. It is made up of several technology-specific societies and publishes hundreds of magazines and thousands of technical journals each year. It also sponsors many conferences and seminars throughout the world. Based in New Jersey, it also maintains a lobbying organization, IEEE-USA, in Washington, D.C.

i-mode   A hugely successful wireless service launched in 1999 by NTT DoCoMo, Japan's largest wireless carrier. The cellular and e-mail/Internet service is accessed via a packet network. Content providers include restaurants, concert ticket brokers, and more than one hundred banks. The service is priced at about three dollars a month. There is also a charge for each transaction, such as a restaurant listing request, or a bank transfer, which is about two or three cents per transaction.

Infrared (IR)   A band of the electromagnetic spectrum commonly used for very short-range (usually less than 10 feet) line-of-sight communications, often for simply exchanging business cards between portable devices. Infrared is familiar to most consumers because it is used for changing channels of TV sets and controlling audio remote devices, and by personal computers with infrared ports for transferring data to a printer.

Infrastructure   This usually refers to the fixed transmitting and receiving equipment in a communications system that sends and receives signals from mobile or handheld subscriber equipment and/or the public switched telephone network (PSTN). It usually consists of a base station, base station controllers, antennas, switches, computers, circuits, and other equipment that make up the backbone of the system.

Instant messaging   Instant messaging enables users to send various types of messages that are delivered in real-time; that is, they are received as they are being sent. This service is very popular in Europe and Japan, but much less so in the United States where wireless subscribers tend to rely more on voice communications. Instant messaging is rapidly evolving to include multimedia content—such as audioclips, videoclips, and images—along with traditional text messaging.

International Mobile Telecommunications 2000 (IMT-2000)   An initiative undertaken by the International Telecommunications Union (ITU) to establish a global standard for third-generation (3G) wireless multimedia communications, including voice, data, Internet, and video.

International Maritime Satellite Organization (Inmarsat)   This London-based organization operates a network of international mobile communications satellites for maritime, aeronautical and land mobile users.

International Telecommunications Satellite Organization (Intelsat) Formed in 1964, Intelsat is an organization of more than one hundred nations that operate a global satellite communication system.

International Telecommunications Union (ITU) An agency of the United Nations, the Geneva-based ITU is responsible for coordinating international telecommunications activities and standards. It usually holds a major meeting, called the World Radiocommunications Conference, every two years.

Internet A very fast-growing global network of linked computer networks that operates by a graphical interface called the World Wide Web. According to a study by the Pew Internet and American Life Project, more than half of all adults in the United States have access to the Internet.

Internet Engineering Task Force (IETF) The IETF is the body that oversees the Internet.

Internet Protocol (IP) Internet Protocol is a communications protocol used by the Internet for transmitting information between various electronic communications devices, such as personal computers and mobile phones. IP is also shorthand for TCP/IP, or Transmission Control Protocol/Internet Protocol.

Interoperability The ability to communicate between varied types of equipment under a single technical standard, or among a variety of compatible local, regional, and national networks.

Intranet An Intranet is an internal or private Internet network that operates within a company, university, or other defined or dedicated organization.

IPv6 (Internet Protocol Version 6) IPv6 is an upgraded version of the Internet Protocol (IP) IPv4. The Internet Engineering Task Force (IETF), the body that oversees the Internet, is developing

IPv6 to replace IPv4, mainly to create more Internet addresses, or numbers, to accommodate the rapid growth of the Internet and, more specifically, the anticipated growth of mobile access of the Internet. One of its key features is a long address field to enable Internet expansion. In addition, security and mobility are built into the protocol.

ISO (International Standards Organization)   The primary international organization for technical standards, including telecommunications.

Java   A programming language for the Internet. Developed by Sun Microsystems, Java software is generally posted on the Web and is downloadable over the Internet to a personal computer or mobile phone.

Keypad   The buttons on the mobile handset.

Kilobits per second (kbps)   One thousand bits per second. The rate at which data can be transmitted.

Kilohertz (kHz)   Equal to a thousand Hertz, or cycles per second.

Legacy system   An information system that is outdated, but which still provides useful service.

LEO   A low-earth-orbit (LEO) mobile communications satellite system (Iridium and Globalstar are two examples) providing global, national, or regional voice and data services. See also Big Leo.

Linux   A UNIX-type operating system originally created by Linus Torvalds. Linux was developed under the GNU General Public License, which means that its source code is available at no charge to everyone.

Location-based   Essentially, the ability to auto-locate mobile users. The application of this technology was initiated by the Federal Communications Commission in 1996 when it ruled that cellular carriers must be able to locate subscribers in emergencies (E-911) within 300 meters of their location by the end of 2001. The ruling will apply to all mobile users by 2005. The term also applies to using mobile "push" technologies, enabling companies to find users and send them material of possible interest rather than waiting for them to request it.

MEO A medium-earth-orbit (MEO) mobile communications satellite, with an orbit of approximately 1800 nautical miles.

Messaging Synonymous with text paging, e-mail, or short messages received on alphanumeric pagers and other wireless devices.

Megahertz (MHz) A measurement of frequency equal to one million Hertz or cycles per second.

Microbrowser Software that lets you access Web pages on a mobile phone. These Web pages are formatted specifically for wireless phones. A microbrowser session is usually started by opening the Menu and scrolling to "Browser." The microbrowser displays the home page set up by your service provider.

Middleware This is communications software that makes it possible for a mobile computer system to communicate with a larger computer or a wireless network. It is designed to "mix and match" diverse radio frequency technologies and technical standards. It was developed in part to encourage applications development by companies using wireless data.

Mobile commerce Also known as m-commerce, this refers to electronic commerce in a mobile environment, using mobile devices to shop or conduct business over the Web.

Mobitex Developed by Ericsson, Mobitex is a cellular land radio-based data communications system used in some two-way packet data networks.

Modem A modem (short for modulate-demodulate) is a device that changes analog signals into digital signals for transmission over analog circuits, or digital signals into analog signals for transmission over analog circuits. Technically, modems modulate discontinuous digital signals into continuous analog waves for transmission over analog circuits and then demodulate the waves into digital bit streams at the receiving end of the circuit.

Motion Picture Experts Group (MPEG)   An industry organization that develops technical standards for downloading film and video for viewing on a desktop PC or mobile device. MPEG4 is a technology for compressing voice, video and related control data and is one of the MPEG's international standards. MPEG4 is expected to be widely incorporated into Third Generation (3G) terminals.

MP3   MP3 is an acronym for MPEG3, which is itself an acronym for Motion Picture Expert Group-1, Audio Layer-3. MPEG defines digital video and audio data compression standards. MP3 lets you download and store music in a digital format. Consumers can legally encode MP3 files from their own CDs, but they cannot legally encode these files and trade them with others without permission of the copyright holder of the music.

Multiapplication   Usually a device that can accommodate more than one application. Some smart cards, for example, can handle multiapplications while maintaining separate security conditions.

Multicarrier code division multiple access (MC-CDMA)   This usually refers to the combination of three IS-95 standard carriers to form one wideband carrier. It is also known as cmda2000, although the formal designation has not yet been set by global standards bodies.

Multimedia   It is the simultaneous use of multiple forms of communications media, such as text, graphics, voice, audio, video, and still images. In practical terms, multimedia refers to having various forms of communications in a single mobile device. A fundamental requirement for supporting multimedia is having enough bandwidth to support multiple applications.

Multimedia Messaging Service (MMS)   MMS can transmit messages containing text, graphics, photographic images, audioclips, and videoclips between WAP-enabled mobile devices. Designed to be used over high-speed GPRS and EDGE transmission systems, MMS is considered to be the next step in mobile-to-mobile messaging, picking up where Short Messaging Service (SMS) leaves off. MMS is specified by both the Third Generation Partnership Project (3GPP) and the Wireless Application Protocol (WAP) Forum. It is also expected to give network operators a new revenue stream from greater airtime when MMS users take advantage of new applications, including wireless advertising.

Number assignment module (NAM)   The NAM is the electronic memory in the wireless phone that stores the telephone number and electronic serial number.

Open systems architecture   An open systems architecture provides for standardized interfaces between telecom switches and radio base stations to facilitate the interconnection of networks produced by different manufacturers.

Operating system   A software program that manages the basic operations of a computer system. These operations include the flow of information into and out of the computer's main processor and to peripherals, and the order and method of handling tasks.

Packet   Data which can be sent or received in packets, or small bursts, over a packet-switched network. It differs from circuit-switching, which involves keeping a circuit open between users for the duration of the connection.

Pager   Small portable receivers that are generally inexpensive and have nationwide coverage. Pagers originated as one-way devices, but two-way paging is available over some networks, notably packet data and narrowband PCS networks.

PAN (Personal Area Network)   Allows devices to work together and share information and services. Using Bluetooth wireless technology, for example, PANs can be created in public places, offices, homes, and cars. PANs also offer the ability to wirelessly synchronize with a desktop computer to access e-mail and Internet or intranet information from remote locations.

PBX (public branch exchange)   A telephone switching system designed to both control and route calls in large multiphone environments, such as offices. Most PBXs can handle custom features for users' specific telecom requirements.

PC Card   A PC Card is a small, credit-card sized plug-in device used to incorporate a variety of peripheral functions into a host computer or other mobile device. It is compatible with the PCMCIA PC Card technical standard. PCMCIA (Personal Computer Memory Card International Association) is an organization that sets technical standards for PC Cards.

PCIA (Personal Communications Industry Association)   A trade association of companies seeking to compete in the global mobile convergence marketplace. Originally dedicated to paging carriers, the PCIA is now focused on advancing seamless global wireless communications.

PCMCIA (Personal Computer Memory Card International Association)   See PC Card.

PCS (Personal Communications Services)   A two-way, personal, digital wireless communications system. Several U.S. cellular companies offer PCS services.

PDA (personal digital assistant)   A handheld computing device for accessing, storing, and organizing information. Newer versions of PDA models can send and receive data wirelessly. Most new PDAs can be used for paging, data messaging, and e-mailing. They also function as electronic organizers (calendars, address books, etc.).

Personal Communications Network (PCN)   A variant of the GSM wireless phone standard. Sometimes called DCS 1800 or GSM 1800.

Personal Communications Services (PCS)   A U.S. variant of the GSM wireless phone standard. Sometimes called GSM 1900.

Personal Handyphone System (PHS)   PHS is Japan's designation for its digital cordless telephony standard. PHS has been in use in

Japan since 1995. It is best suited for use in densely populated urban areas by pedestrians; however, because of the design of its system architecture, it does not work well from moving vehicles.

Personalization   A concept of developing features for mobile devices that are of use and interest to a specific user, such as unique location-based services, restaurant listings, or reports on specific stock quotations. Also, a process by which a smart card is modified to contain the information for one person. Graphical personalization modifies the visual aspect of the card (holder's name, photograph, etc.).

Personal trusted device   A device that has been authenticated.

PIM (Personal Information Manager)   Although sometimes referred to as personal digital assistant (PDA), PIM is a software application for organizing personal information. Most PIMs offer the capability to record and access personal notes, lists, dates, and calculator programs.

PIN (Personal Identification Number)   The number or code that mobile subscribers or cardholders would use to confirm their identity.

Portal   A site on the Internet that people often visit, such as America Online (AOL) or Yahoo!

POS (point of sale)   POS terminals are handheld or desktop devices (including cash registers) that can conduct transactions with smart (including credit) cards. The terminals are usually linked to a central computer, either wired or wirelessly.

Presence services   Presence service provides a system for sharing personal information about the user's status (online, offline, busy), and location (office, home). It enables users to subscribe to presence such as listings of which colleagues and friends are currently online. In addition, these services enable users to participate in private or public chat rooms with search capabilities. Ultimately, network operators will be able to provide meeting and conferencing services with shared content.

Protocol   A protocol is a set of standard rules that define and govern how a computer or communication system processes data for transmission across a network. Protocols describe both the format that a message must take and the way in which messages are exchanged between communications devices and computers. Protocols are usually defined by a published technical standard or reference.

Public key infrastructure (PKI)   PKI is based on public key cryptographic techniques. It enables the use of public key encryption and digital certificates in a distributed computer network and is used to ensure authentic and private communications over the Internet. PKI technology is expected to be integrated into more mobile applications and operating systems, particularly with the development and growth of mobile commerce applications and activities.

Public safety answering point (PSAP)   The dispatch office that receives 911 calls from the public. A PSAP may be a local fire or police department, an emergency medical service, or a regional office covering all of these services.

Public switched telephone network (PSTN)   The worldwide telecommunications network used by everyone with telephone service.

Pull technology   Technology used to locate and download information to a computer or other mobile device. It differs from push technology in that pull information must be requested by the subscriber or user.

Push technology   Technology that enables information, such as news headlines, or "wireless ads," to be sent automatically to a computer on a random or regular basis—for example, hourly. This technology is somewhat controversial in that wireless service subscribers or mobile device users receive information without actually having requested it.

Radio frequency (RF)   In terms of cellular communications, RF is that part of the electromagnetic spectrum between the audio and high-range frequencies (between 500 kHz and 300 GHz). Cellular transmission frequencies are found in two locations in the spectrum—at 824–849 MHz and 869–894 MHz.

Radio frequency identification (RFID)   RFID tags, which can be smaller than a button on a jacket, have a unique electronic signature and can be attached to almost anything for tracking and monitoring valuable assets, such as large crates or small packages. Most RFID tags transmit a constant signal. The U.S. military is a major user of RFID technology. It also has wide use commercially; laundries, for example, have used RFID tags to locate and identify shirts that have been mixed up in a pile.

Roaming   A service offered by most cellular service providers that allows subscribers to use cellular service while traveling outside their home service area.

Second Generation mobile telecommunications (2G)   2G systems used in the United States usually combine analog and digital (dual-mode) and provide voice/data, fax transmissions along with other services. Currently, 2G systems are evolving into what have become known as 2.5G devices, with increasing data rates via high-speed circuit-switched data and General Packet Radio Service.

SET (Secure Electronic Transaction)   SET is an open technical standard for commerce developed by MasterCard and Visa protocol as a way to facilitate secure payment card transactions over the Internet. SET relies on cryptography and digital certificates to ensure message confidentiality. With SET, merchants never have access to the customer's card number, thus limiting potential fraud.

Short Messaging Service (SMS)   Much more popular in Europe and Japan than in the United States, SMS is used for sending short text messages of up to 160 characters between mobile subscribers. As the technology has evolved, a number of services have been introduced, including e-mail, fax, paging integration, interactive banking, information services such as stock quotes, and integration with Internet-based applications. SMS is not available in all areas.

SIM   See Subscriber identity module (SIM).

Smart card   A plastic card with an embedded microprocessor and/or memory chip for storing information, usually for identification and financial transactions. See *also* Subscriber identity module (SIM).

Smart phone   A cellular phone that can connect to the Internet, send and receive e-mail, and which often has additional advanced features similar to those available in a personal digital assistant (PDA) or an electronic organizer.

Specialized Mobile Radio (SMR)   A private, business service using mobile radiotelephones and base stations to communicate via the public phone network.

Spectrum   The complete range of electromagnetic waves that make up the radio frequencies (RF) assigned to specific communication services, such as cellular, paging, and satellites. These waves vary in length. Longer waves in the low-frequency range can be used for communications, whereas shorter waves of very high frequency show up as light.

Spread spectrum   Originally developed by the U.S. military for secure communications, spread spectrum radio transmissions essentially "spread" a radio signal over a very wide frequency band in order to make it difficult to intercept or jam. Spread spectrum techniques are becoming widely used in a number of commercial communications applications. Code division multiple access (CDMA), the transmission technique used by many cellular phones, particularly in the United States, is based on spread spectrum techniques.

Standard   A standard is a set of technical specifications defining the physical, electrical, or logical properties of a device. Mobile device standard-setting bodies include the ISO and ETSI.

Streaming   A one-way transmission of video and/or audio over the Internet. Streaming can be sent over advanced wideband wireless networks without waiting for an entire "file" to be downloaded—

hence, streaming. Streaming can be transmitted point-to-point or broadcast from an origination point to multiple receivers.

Subscriber identity module (SIM)   A plastic smart card that contains personal subscriber-related data for accessing a network, mainly for billing purposes. It can be installed or inserted into a mobile phone, similar to how credit cards are "swiped" in cash registers.

Symbian   A company created jointly by Psion, Nokia, Ericsson, Motorola, and Matsushita in June 1998 to develop and standardize a mobile phone operating system known as EPOC. Symbian is promoting EPOC as an interoperable standard for portable phones of different manufacturers.

Synchronization   The process of uploading and downloading information from two or more databases, so that each is identical. For example, synchronization techniques can be used for moving business or personal data from a personal digital assistant (PDA) to a desktop computer.

T1   The transmission rate of 1.544 megabits per second (mbps), or the equivalent of the ISDN Primary Rate Interface for the United States.

TDMA (time division multiple access)   TDMA is a digital cellular platform that converts audio signals into digital information (0s and 1s) and divides them into digital packets. The packets are then transmitted on a single radio frequency. TDMA differs from CDMA in that it uses one channel instead of several and has about a third of the channel capacity of CDMA.

Telecommunications Act of 1996   Signed into law by President Clinton on February 8, 1996, the Telecom Act established a pro-competitive, deregulatory framework for telecommunications in the United States.

Telecommunications Industry Association (TIA)   TIA is a U.S.-based association of telecommunications and information technology companies involved in standards development and promoting international business opportunities for its members. The TIA represents the communications sector of the Electronic Industries Alliance (EIA).

Telematics	The integration of mobile communications and information technologies, mainly for vehicle navigation, monitoring systems, and location devices.

Telemetry	A wireless or landline system for the transmission of data (either digital or analog) for remote monitoring.

Terminal	A term used in the telecom industry for a phone. Also can be a networked desktop computer.

TETRA (Terrestrial Trunked Radio)	The European trunked radio system, similar to the Specialized Mobile Radio (SMR) system in the United States, which is used mainly as a dispatch radio service.

Third Generation mobile telecommunications (3G)	A new and evolving technical standard designed to offer increased capacity and high-speed data applications. It will also enable global roaming. The Wireless Administrative Radio Conference has assigned 230 megahertz (MHz) of spectrum for multimedia 3G networks. The International Telecommunications Union (ITU) hopes to coordinate this next-generation standard through its International Mobile Telecommunications-2000 (ITU-2000) program. Third Generation specifications are being finalized by the 3G Partnership Project (3GPP). However, Japan and Europe have already decided to adopt WCDMA-DS in an attempt to get a lead in advanced mobile services.

Third-Generation Partnership Project (3GPP)	3GPP is a global body dedicated to the development of 3G specifications.

Transceiver	A two-way radio that combines a transmitter and a receiver in a single unit.

Transmission Control Protocol/Internet Protocol (TCP/IP)	A protocol that governs communications among all computers on the Internet. TCP/IP is a set of instructions that dictates how packets of information are sent across multiple networks.

Tri-band   A wireless phone that offers both dual-mode and dual-band capability to enhance its geographic service area. Dual-mode allows the phone to access digital and AMP (analog) channels. Similarly, dual-band enables a mobile phone to operate on two digital frequencies. For example, a dual-band phone could operate on both 800 MHz CDMA and 1900 MHz GSM digital networks. These are network and subscription dependent features. They are not available in all areas.

Two-way pager   A pager that enables the user to reply to a message and originate messages or e-mail.

UHF (Ultra high frequency)   Radio channels operating in the 300 MHz to 3 GHz range.

UMTS Terrestrial Radio Access (UTRA)   Usually defined as the same as wideband code division multiple access, or, more precisely, WCDMA-DS.

Universal Mobile Telecommunications System (UMTS)   The European term for Third Generation (3G) telecommunications system based on the IMT-2000 standard.

Universal Wireless Communications Consortium (UWCC)   UWCC is a U.S.-based international consortium of wireless carriers and vendors supporting TDMA, EDGE, UMTS, and WIN technical standards.

User interface   The means by which the user interacts with the device. This can be a keyboard, dedicated function buttons, or displays.

Virtual private network (VPN)   VPNs, or Internet Protocol (IP) VPNs, can provide all the capabilities of a private network, delivered over a carrier's shared IP network facilities. The key elements of a VPN include switching, record creation and record keeping, customer premise equipment, and an access arrangement for connecting a corporate customer to the carrier's network. Wireless VPNs that are now becoming available allow users of supported mobile devices to securely connect to their corporate networks through their existing VPN gateways to make use of their intranet resources.

Voice activation   A feature that allows a subscriber to dial a phone number by spoken commands.

Voice mail   Also called voice messaging, this is a computerized answering service that allows mobile phone subscribers to record voice messages. The more sophisticated of these services can notify subscribers, via a pager, that they have received a call.

Voice pager   A pager that can receive and play back voice messages.

Voice portal   Voice portals are Internet services that enable users to access information using speech recognition technology, usually through a hardwired connection. Since so many new mobile applications are in development, most analysts believe that mobile voice portal use will begin to surpass fixed wired connections in 2003.

Voice recognition   Also referred to as speech recognition, this is a technology that enables users to activate and/or control the functions of their cellular phones and other electronic devices by voice commands.

WAP (Wireless Application Protocol)   A standard that aims to align industry efforts to bring advanced applications and Internet content to digital cellular phones and other digital wireless devices.

WCDMA (wideband code division multiple access)   Also known as WCMDA-DS (for direct sequence), this is a radio interface for the Third Generation (3G) Universal Mobile Telephone System (UMTS). WCDMA will be used to provide the type of services currently performed by the GSM cellular network. It transmits at speeds up to 2 mbps and is fully compliant with IMT-2000 for 3G services.

WIM (WAP Identity Module)   A subscriber identity module (SIM) that is specifically developed for the mobile Internet.

Wireless Administrative Radio Conference (WARC)   A series of meetings held every two years by International Telecommunications Union (ITU) member nations to negotiate global spectrum allocation and related issues.

Wireless Application Service Provider (WASP)   WASPs generally provide turnkey wireless data and mobile commerce services for wireless carriers, e-businesses and corporations. These services include application development and implementation, strategic planning, hosting and marketing services, content and mobile commerce development and distribution, portal and platform development, and customer service.

Wireless Internet   A radio-based service that provides access to e-mail and/or the World Wide Web.

Wireless Internet Service Provider (WISP)   Typically, you gain access to the Internet though an Internet service provider. ISPs, as they are more simply known, make the connection from your office or home to a central computer, or server, which then makes the connection to the Internet. Wireless ISPs do essentially the same thing, but in a mobile environment.

Wireless Local Area Network (WLAN)   A network that allows the transfer of data and the ability to share resources, such as printers, without the need to physically connect each node, or computer, with wires.

Wireless Markup Language (WML)   WML is an open standard markup language developed specifically for wireless applications. It is part of the Wireless Application Protocol (WAP), and is based on the Extensible Markup Language (XML).

Index